Daily Wisdom

3-MINUTE DEVOTIONS FOR WOMEN

Daily Wisdom

3-MINUTE DEVOTIONS
FOR WOMEN

Carol Lynn Fitzpatrick

BARBOUR BOOKS
An Imprint of Barbour Publishing, Inc.

Print ISBN 978-1-63409-689-8

eBook Editions:
Adobe Digital Edition (.epub) 978-1-63409-691-1
Kindle and MobiPocket Edition (.prc) 978-1-63409-690-4

Published by Barbour Books, an imprint of Barbour Publishing, Inc., P.O. Box 719, Uhrichsville, Ohio 44683, www.barbourbooks.com

Our mission is to publish and distribute inspirational products offering exceptional value and biblical encouragement to the masses.

 Member of the
Evangelical Christian
Publishers Association

Printed in the United States of America.

Introduction

In Christ alone we find the wisdom we seek:

> *But by His doing you are in Christ Jesus, who became to us wisdom from God, and righteousness and sanctification, and redemption, so that, just as it is written, "LET HIM WHO BOASTS, BOAST IN THE LORD."*
> 1 CORINTHIANS 1:30–31

Since its first release nearly two decades ago, the devotional *Daily Wisdom for Women* has become a perennial favorite, touching the lives of more than 750,000 readers. This carefully edited, brand-new "3-Minute Devotions" edition includes the very best readings in an easy-to-use, just-right-size format:

Minute 1: Meditate on the scripture selection.

Minute 2: Read the brief devotional reading.

Minute 3: Use the prayer as a springboard for your own time of talking with God.

May this beautiful collection encourage your heart as you seek the true wisdom found only in God's Word.

Be blessed!

—The Editors

In the Garden

When the woman saw that the tree was good for food,
and that it was a delight to the eyes, and that the tree was
desirable to make one wise, she took from its fruit and ate;
and she gave also to her husband with her, and he ate.

GENESIS 3:6

Eve stood beside the "tree of the knowledge of good and evil" and began listening to the seductive voice of the crafty serpent.

And Adam, who loved her, listened to her voice and joined her in eating the fruit of the tree. As a result, Adam and Eve were forced out of this physical garden paradise. Yet the echo of God's loving promise lingered in their ears. . . . A Redeemer would come.

Thousands of years later, Jesus prayed in another garden. And His sacrifice on the cross provided forgiveness, once again allowing access to God's presence. . .now within a spiritual garden of prayer.

Lord, I know I have walked away from You at some point of sin. That's why You sent Jesus to be my Savior. Forgive me, and enable me with Your strength to run from sin and toward prayer.

Seeking Wisdom

To receive instruction in wise behavior...to the youth knowledge and discretion, a wise man will hear and increase in learning, and a man of understanding will acquire wise counsel, to understand a proverb and a figure, the words of the wise and their riddles.

PROVERBS 1:3–6

When asked by God what he wished for, Solomon answered, "Wisdom." If you'd been asked this question in your early twenties, what would your response have been?

Seventeen-year-old Natalie found the advances of an older man extremely difficult to resist. Disregarding everything she'd learned in Sunday school, Natalie turned instead to a non-Christian girlfriend for advice. "Go for it!" the friend encouraged with gusto.

A decade later that friend has been married and divorced. Natalie herself found out too late that her "boyfriend" already had a wife and baby.

Satan still finds his way into vulnerable areas of our lives. But God is with you, even in times of temptation. He'll give you the power and wisdom to withstand such moral crises.

Lord, surround me with friends who know You and Your Word. Surround me in a crisis so I can hear Your voice of wisdom.

Fishers of Men

"Come, follow me," Jesus said, "and I will
send you out to fish for people."
MATTHEW 4:19 NIV

When He spoke the words recorded above, Peter and
Andrew must have been intrigued. But Jesus didn't invent
the phrase "fishers of men." Philosophers and teachers of
that day used this term to describe those who captured
men's minds.

Why did Christ want these fishermen? Peter and
Andrew were men of action who knew how to get a job
done without quitting or complaining. Their tenacity
would be an asset to Christ's ministry of soul winning.

Jesus came not only to save but to teach men and
women how to have true servants' hearts. The substance of
ministry is service.

Lord, show me clearly where I can be of service within
my local body of believers. Perhaps there's a small
hand in the Sunday school just waiting to be held.

Vocalizing a Prayer

"And when you are praying, do not use meaningless repetition as the Gentiles do, for they suppose that they will be heard for their many words."

MATTHEW 6:7

If you can remember the acrostic ACTS, you'll have an excellent formula for prayer: Adoration, Confession, Thanksgiving, and Supplication.

As we come before the Lord, we first need to honor Him as Creator, Master, Savior, and Lord. Reflect on who He is and praise Him. And because we're human, we need to confess and repent of our daily sins. Following this, we should be in a mode of thanksgiving. Finally, our prayer requests should be upheld.

Your prayers certainly don't have to be elaborate or polished. God does not judge your way with words. He knows your heart. He wants to hear from you.

Lord, Your Word says that my prayers rise up to heaven like incense from the earth. Remind me daily to send a sweet savor Your way!

Turn Your Ear to Wisdom

*For the LORD gives wisdom; from His mouth come
knowledge and understanding. He stores up sound
wisdom for the upright; He is a shield to those who
walk in integrity, guarding the paths of justice,
and He preserves the way of His godly ones.*
PROVERBS 2:6–8

Every family has at least one relative who cannot get his act together.

Are you smiling yet? Is someone in particular coming clearly into focus? Now, hold that thought.

God's Word says wisdom is truly a gift since it comes from the mouth of God, from the very words He speaks. And all God's words have been written down for us through the inspiration of the Holy Spirit. Therefore, those who refuse to accept God's guidance, who refuse to ask for His wisdom—those hapless relatives, perhaps—will never see the light of reality.

Know that if you hold fast to the precepts contained in the Bible, you will walk in integrity. Your feet will be planted on the straight and narrow road.

Lord, I can't change my relatives, but I can change myself. Please give me Your guidance and wisdom.

False Prophets

"Beware of the false prophets, who come to you in sheep's clothing, but inwardly are ravenous wolves. You will know them by their fruits. Grapes are not gathered from thorn bushes nor figs from thistles, are they?"

MATTHEW 7:15–16

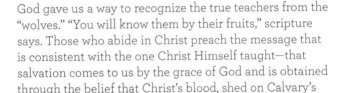

God gave us a way to recognize the true teachers from the "wolves." "You will know them by their fruits," scripture says. Those who abide in Christ preach the message that is consistent with the one Christ Himself taught—that salvation comes to us by the grace of God and is obtained through the belief that Christ's blood, shed on Calvary's cross, has cleansed us from our sin.

Don't be afraid to ask questions. True teachers will always be pleased to give straightforward answers.

Lord, there are so many voices. Please help us to hear Yours so that we won't be led astray by the wolves in sheep's clothing who make a mockery out of Your great sacrifice for us.

A Furious Storm

*When He got into the boat, His disciples followed Him.
And behold, there arose a great storm on the sea, so that
the boat was being covered with the waves; but Jesus
Himself was asleep. And they came to Him and woke
Him, saying, "Save us, Lord; we are perishing!"*

MATTHEW 8:23–25

The disciples were in the midst of a storm. Yet Jesus was with them in the boat. They woke Him in the throes of panic, sure that the waves would swallow them up. Jesus took the disciples to the height of the storm's raging fury, yet all the time He was with them. Later on in this chapter, Jesus rose up and rebuked the winds and sea and everything became perfectly calm. Yes, the storms of life will attempt to ravage me, but Christ is there amid the frenzy, ready to deliver by just the power of His Word. He will carry me safely to the other side of the shore.

*Lord, keep my eyes focused not on the storms of life,
but on Your awesome power to deliver me from them.*

King Forever and Ever

The LORD is King forever and ever;
nations have perished from His land.

PSALM 10:16

Satan, whose dominion is the world, has devoted all his efforts to eradicating Christianity. Yet, while the evil one's influence can seem as ugly as any ink stain, Satan's mark on this earth will not be permanent. The reason? God's Son, Jesus Christ, lives forever within those who call upon His name. And despite the efforts of the evil one, Jesus will remain King and one day soon will come back to claim this earth for His own, forever and ever.

Are you assured of your place in Christ's kingdom?

Lord, as this world becomes increasingly evil, reflecting the one who holds its "title deed," remind me that You're coming back to claim all that is rightfully Yours.

Who Are the Faithful?

Help, LORD, for the godly man ceases to be, for the faithful disappear from among the sons of men.

PSALM 12:1

Who are the faithful? They are the ones who continue to follow God no matter what obstacles are thrown in their path. One of the faithful, a dear friend who has debilitating multiple sclerosis, is one of the most joyful Christians I know.

Another friend has led a Bible study for years, despite the fact that her husband is frequently out of work and their finances are at times nearly nonexistent.

By now you have probably decided that it doesn't pay to become one of my friends. But I must reassure you that neither of these women consider shrinking back from following Christ. Instead, they agree with the apostle Paul that these present circumstances and trials are but "light and momentary" compared with the peace we will have in Christ for all eternity (2 Corinthians 4:17).

Lord, I have watched people carry burdens that, humanly speaking, should be unbearable. Yet with these trials You give them incredible joy. I praise You for all You are!

A Great Light

The people who walk in darkness will see a great light;
those who live in a dark land, the light will shine on them.

ISAIAH 9:2

The Israelites had no idea that such a great depth of darkness had overtaken them until they were in the midst of it. God previously had provided them with great light, for He communicated directly with their leaders. But the Israelites chose to act as though the switch of truth had never been turned on. They were caught up in the dark snare of idolatry.

Are you refusing to act on God's insight, insisting on pursuits that distract you from worshipping Him? How we spend our time is but a habit, and habits can be changed by making a new pattern for our actions. Walk in the light, as your Father intended.

Lord, change the desire of my heart to seek and know
You better. Take my life and use me for Your purposes.

Our Advocate and Defender

"Therefore everyone who confesses Me before men,
I will also confess him before My Father who is in heaven."

MATTHEW 10:32

Busy with friends her own age, my older sister didn't usually accompany my younger sister and me on our morning trek to school.

However, when we returned home one day relating that two big kids had threatened to beat us up the next day, she rallied to the cause. As she instructed, we traversed our normal route while she lagged watchfully a short distance behind.

Suddenly, the two boys jumped out of the bushes ahead. And just like a superwoman, our sister pounced on them, easily overpowering both and giving them bloody noses in the process. It felt so incredible to have an invincible defender!

If we know Jesus Christ and have responded to His invitation to receive Him as Savior, Jesus remains forever our advocate. Know that you are so precious to Jesus that He gave His life for you. Doesn't it feel amazing to have Jesus as your defender?

Lord, how reassuring it is to know You mightily defend not only my body but also my soul against attack.

Joseph Honors God

Now Joseph was well-built and handsome,
and after a while his master's wife took notice of
Joseph and said, "Come to bed with me!" But he refused.
GENESIS 39:6–8 NIV

Joseph could neither dishonor Potiphar, an Egyptian officer of Pharaoh, nor disobey his God. But day after day Potiphar's wife kept after Joseph, hoping to wear down his resistance. But when Joseph's outer garment fell away as he fled, she proceeded to act like a scorned woman and had Joseph thrown into jail.

But God had a plan. Through an incredible chain of events, Joseph was found innocent and released from prison after he correctly interpreted the king's disturbing dream. Eventually Joseph's position was restored, and he created a stockpile of grain that saw both Egypt and Joseph's restored family through a great famine—the one he had predicted in that dream.

Joseph's moral stand preserved the very ancestral line leading up to Jesus Christ.

Lord, I can't look ahead to see how a critical moment of obedience fits into Your overall plan. Please give me Your strength when my human desires threaten to overpower me.

Why Jesus Spoke in Parables

*And the disciples came and said to Him,
"Why do You speak to them in parables?"*
MATTHEW 13:10

Jesus' main purpose in coming to earth was to communicate God's love by His perfect words and actions. Certainly He could clearly articulate a point when He desired. So why did He shroud many of His teachings behind a veil of curious stories?

Jesus Himself explains: "Therefore I speak to them in parables; because while seeing they do not see, and while hearing they do not hear, nor do they understand'" (Matthew 13:13). Who was Jesus talking about? Only moments before, He'd been conversing with the scribes and Pharisees. And although they had great knowledge of God's Word, they refused to see its very fulfillment before their eyes. Everything Jesus did and said confirmed that He was their long-awaited Messiah. Yet they closed their eyes and stopped up their ears.

Yet to those who He knew would respond, He provided plain words. How open have you been to God's Word?

Lord, Your truth surrounds me. Please lift my eyelids to see it and stir my heart to respond to Your Word.

Rescued from My Enemies

He reached down from on high and took hold of me;
he drew me out of deep waters. He rescued me from my
powerful enemy, from my foes, who were too strong for
me. They confronted me in the day of my disaster,
but the LORD was my support.

PSALM 18:16–18 NIV

David wrote this psalm at a time when he was being
pursued by Saul. Imagine David's terror as he and his band
of loyal followers huddled within the concealing walls
of caves for shelter while Saul sought to slaughter him.
During this time of desperation, David learned to lean on
God's power, convinced in his heart that He alone could
rescue him from harm.

Have you ever known such desperation? Did you
realize that He could act in your behalf, despite the obvious
circumstances?

The very character of God demands that He rescue
those whom He loves. When confronted with a crisis, like
David, you can put your life in His hands.

Lord, when all is lost, I thank You that You
reach out to me with Your mighty hand of rescue.
Your welcoming hand is a lifeline in any storm.

Trials Have a Purpose

Then Joseph said to his brothers, "Please come closer to me." And they came closer. And he said, "I am your brother Joseph, whom you sold into Egypt. Now do not be grieved or angry with yourselves, because you sold me here, for God sent me before you to preserve life."

GENESIS 45:4–5

How many of us could forgive as Joseph did? His jealous siblings kidnapped him, threw him into a pit, and then allowed him to be sold into slavery. Yet Joseph trusted that from God's perspective—not his own—his trials had a purpose.

Is there a hurt so deep inside that you have never shared it with another human being? Perhaps someone in your own family has rejected or betrayed you. Remember the pain suffered by Joseph; remember the anguish of Jesus Christ, who was betrayed by one as close as a brother, Judas Iscariot. God knows your pain and He is strong enough to remove any burden.

Lord, sometimes I want to enjoy my agony a while longer. Show me the brilliance of Your forgiveness that I might trust You in the trial and not miss the outcome You've planned.

A Life Turned Around

The man said, "Who made you ruler and judge over
us? Are you thinking of killing me as you killed the
Egyptian?" Then Moses was afraid and thought,
"What I did must have become known."

EXODUS 2:14 NIV

Moses had killed an Egyptian. Was it right? No. God
Himself administers true justice, in His own time, to those
who deserve punishment.

Later, God revealed His plan to Moses, a plan to bring
the Israelites out of Egypt. So when Moses asks God, "Who
am I that I should go to Pharaoh and bring the Israelites
out of Egypt?" it comes from the heart of one who has
murdered and knows his guilt before God. But instead of
rebuke Moses hears, "I will be with you. . . . I AM WHO I AM"
(Exodus 3:11–12, 14 NIV). This is the same "I AM" who calls
you to serve Him today.

Lord, Moses felt unworthy to serve You because of his
great sin. Forgive me of my sins and focus my life on You.

Who Is Christ to You?

"But what about you?" Jesus asked. "Who do you say I am?"
Simon Peter answered, "You are the Messiah,
the Son of the living God."
MATTHEW 16:15–16 NIV

Jesus knew that once He was gone His followers would be scattered and most would die for their faith in Him. Therefore, it was crucial that they understand exactly who Christ was.

Six days after this conversation with Peter, a miraculous event occurred. Jesus took Peter, James, and John up a high mountain. And there He was transfigured before them. "His face shone like the sun, and his clothes became as white as the light" (Matthew 17:2 NIV). Moses and Elijah appeared with Jesus and spoke with Him.

A bright cloud overshadowed them and a voice from heaven said, "This is my Son, whom I love; with him I am well pleased. Listen to him!" (17:5). Just the awesome sound of God's voice caused the disciples to fall on their faces in fear.

Jesus Christ, Son of God, Son of Man, Redeemer, displayed His glory to these disciples. Do you know Him as Savior?

Lord, let me declare, as Peter did,
"You are the Christ, the Son of God."

Forsaken by God?

My God, my God, why have You forsaken me?
Far from my deliverance are the words of my groaning.

PSALM 22:1

Have you ever cried out to God with such despair? I have. While my clenched fists beat against my bedroom wall, twelve years' worth of tears—a maelstrom of anger, hurt, and frustration—flowed freely.

He showed me the cross. The year was 1973. I left my knapsack of grief on the bloodstained ground beneath His wooden cross. And I never looked back. He has met my every need in surprising, miraculous, and incredible ways.

Jesus, separated from the Father because of our sin, reached the ear of God with His own desperation. He experienced for us this ultimate terror. . .so that we would never be forsaken or walk alone on the road that leads to Calvary.

Where are you? On the road, walking toward Him? Sitting down, too bewildered to even formulate questions? Or are you kneeling, as I did, right at His bleeding feet?

Lord, no matter what hazards are down the road,
You've got a signpost ready to hang on whatever
misleading marker is already in the ground.
And the Son is shining ahead!

Fit for Service

*Then Moses said to the LORD, "Please, Lord, I have
never been eloquent, neither recently nor in time
past, nor since You have spoken to Your servant;
for I am slow of speech and slow of tongue."*

EXODUS 4:10

Moses heard God's voice clearly calling him to this
position. Why was he balking at the task?

Remember that Moses was nothing but a murderer
with the best of intentions when God first met him at that
burning bush. Perhaps he took a momentary look back at
his life before the Lord got hold of him.

The passage continues: "Then the anger of the LORD
burned against Moses, and He said, 'Is there not your
brother Aaron the Levite.... He shall speak for you to the
people'" (Exodus 4:14, 16). Now, if this were God's plan all
along, why was He angry with Moses? Because the Lord
wanted Moses to understand that He could and would
meet all of his needs.

*Lord, I am inadequate to understand Your perfection.
Please help me see that Your help is like owning a store that
has everything I need in utterly limitless supply.*

Pharaoh Admits His Sin

Then Pharaoh sent for Moses and Aaron, and said to them,
"I have sinned this time; the LORD is the righteous one,
and I and my people are the wicked ones."

EXODUS 9:27

One would think that with an admission like this, especially from an unbelieving ruler, the man had finally seen the light. Pharaoh sounds ready to commit his heart and soul to the almighty God. Wrong!

Pharaoh's heart had not yielded to God's authority. Three more plagues would come upon the people because their leader refused to honor the true God.

Pharaoh would pay a terrible price for his sins. In the end, his stubbornness would cause the loss of his own precious son. This would be the final curse in Egypt, the death of every firstborn son.

Lord, it's so easy to see Pharaoh's obstinate
streak. Give me strength to admit when
I'm wrong. Give me strength to come
to You in repentance.

Renewal of All Things

Then Peter said to Him, "Behold, we have left everything and followed You; what then will there be for us?"
And Jesus said to them, "Truly I say to you, that you who have followed Me, in the regeneration when the Son of Man will sit on His glorious throne, you also shall sit upon twelve thrones, judging the twelve tribes of Israel."

MATTHEW 19:27–28

Peter was saying, "Lord, when we get to the end, will it have been worth it to follow You?" And Jesus reassures him with a gigantic yes!

The Lord went a step further and related that Peter not only would be with Christ, the Son of Man, eternally, but he would have work to do once he arrived in heaven.

None of us will just occupy space in heaven. Our God is always productive.

Have you ever speculated as to what you might do in heaven? Well, don't worry—the tasks you perform will be custom-tailored to you.

Lord, I can't even imagine what You have in store for me in heaven. Please keep me faithful to complete the duties You've called me to on earth.

The Passover Lamb

"Slay the Passover lamb. You shall take a bunch of hyssop and dip it in the blood which is in the basin, and apply some of the blood that is in the basin to the lintel and the two doorposts; and none of you shall go outside the door of his house until morning. For the LORD will pass through to smite the Egyptians; and when He sees the blood on the lintel and on the two doorposts, the LORD will pass over the door and will not allow the destroyer to come in to your houses to smite you."

EXODUS 12:21–23

This scripture passage paints a comprehensive picture of the Passover.

Each year this symbolic Passover meal is re-created.

We can celebrate the Passover with joy and thanksgiving, knowing for certain that the long-awaited Messiah has come and will come again!

Lord Jesus Christ, I thank You for being my promised Messiah and Passover Lamb. I thank You for Your sacrifice so that my sins could be forgiven.

An Invitation to Dine

"The kingdom of heaven may be compared to a king who gave a wedding feast for his son."

MATTHEW 22:2

When God sent His Son to earth, He invited all men and women to a wedding feast. Those who accept the invitation become part of the Church. And the Church is the bride of Christ.

The Son is the Bridegroom for whom the wedding feast is prepared. God Himself has laid the groundwork in the hearts that will respond to His Son, Jesus Christ.

There will be an appointed hour in the future when the guests will come to the banquet. And Christ will call them forth to be His Church when all is made ready, after His resurrection and ascension and the coming of the Holy Spirit at Pentecost.

Also, those in attendance receive "wedding clothes." Jesus Christ now clothes them in His righteousness. Those not wearing these garments are cast out because they refused Christ's invitation and, in so doing, have rejected His salvation.

Lord, You've invited me to dine with You.
Let me graciously accept my "wedding clothes."

Remember the Sabbath

*"Remember the sabbath day, to keep it holy. Six days you
shall labor and do all your work, but the seventh day
is a sabbath of the LORD your God; in it you
shall not do any work."*

EXODUS 20:8–11

During the 1950s in Missouri where I grew up, blue laws
virtually shut down the city on Sundays. Merchants finally
managed to get these laws overturned, and the stores
opened on Sunday. Sales were timed to begin early on the
Sabbath, enticing people to make a choice between church
and shopping. On a Sunday morning, compare the number
of cars at the mall with those at church. This worldly
strategy has certainly been effective.

In the very beginning of our marriage, my husband
and I made a decision to honor God on Sunday. He
has blessed our family over and over for this faithful
commitment, not only providing the weekly spiritual
guidance we desperately need, but also giving our bodies
and souls the rest they require.

*Lord, please help me to remember that
Your commandments are always for my good.*

Mourning Turned into Dancing

You have turned for me my mourning into dancing.

PSALM 30:11

Years ago I was drawn to watch Corrie ten Boom one day on television. She spoke about a meeting, long after World War II, with the SS soldier who had stood guard in the showers at her concentration camp. When I heard her speak about extending her hand in a gesture of forgiveness, her words pierced through my soul like a dagger. How could she offer the hand of friendship to him? Lacking her own strength, Corrie prayed to God for Him to give His forgiveness to this man. And when Corrie's hand touched the former soldier's, she likened it to love's lightning going through her arm, to the man, and then back again.

At the time, there were many people whom I felt incapable of pardoning. God's name topped the list. Corrie's words lingered in my mind and heart, making me miserable. But I finally surrendered my life to Christ. And God's power of forgiveness has turned my own mourning into dancing.

Lord, Your "merry saint," Corrie, knew joy was a condition of a heart filled with forgiveness. Help me see this, too!

Peter's Denial

Then Jesus said to them, "You will all fall away because of Me this night, for it is written, 'I WILL STRIKE DOWN THE SHEPHERD, AND THE SHEEP OF THE FLOCK SHALL BE SCATTERED.' But after I have been raised, I will go ahead of you to Galilee." But Peter said to Him, "Even though all may fall away because of You, I will never fall away."

MATTHEW 26:31-33

Peter was convinced that his faith in Christ was so strong nothing could cause it to crumble. Yet only a few hours later, he cowered when a young servant girl accused him of being one of Jesus' followers. And then he openly denied his Lord.

There have been times when you have disappointed Jesus. Have you asked for forgiveness? Have you realized that upon asking, the burden of sin will be lifted forever?

Lord, I have, at one time or another, acted as if I could live any way I wanted. Yet it cost Christ everything to purchase my redemption. Let me willingly come and pray to You.

Before He Set the Heavens in Place

*"The LORD possessed me at the beginning of His way,
before His works of old. From everlasting I was established,
from the beginning, from the earliest times of the earth.
When there were no depths I was brought forth, when
there were no springs abounding with water.... When He
marked out the foundations of the earth; then I
was beside Him, as a master workman."*

PROVERBS 8:22–24, 29–30

What existed before anything else? God. And now woman
and man come along, filling in a narrow blip of time, and
state that all of creation "just simply evolved." Get a clue!
God designed, planned, and implemented all that we do
see and everything we can't comprehend.

Somehow we have turned around history. Humans are
not in charge. God is. And He's still commanding the dawn
to happen and the earth to keep spinning and the stars to
remain in the sky. Aren't you glad?

*Lord, keep me from taking Your magnificence for granted.
Let my heart overflow with gratitude for all You are.*

Offerings for the Tent of Meeting

Then the whole Israelite community withdrew from Moses'
presence, and everyone who was willing and whose heart
moved them came and brought an offering to the LORD
for the work on the tent of meeting, for all its
service, and for the sacred garments.

EXODUS 35:20–21 NIV

When was the last time your whole community agreed on anything? Imagine everyone's talents, skills, and resources united for a common purpose!

The hearts of God's people were stirred to erect the tent of meeting, following the Lord's command. Leaving all selfish desires behind, they pooled their brooches, earrings, signet rings, bracelets, and other offerings of gold for the Lord. From these articles gemstones were extracted to make the ephod and the breastplate.

As those in Moses' day brought all they possessed, we can surrender our own time and talents.

How is God using you in His Church?

Lord, You've created within me something to be used to
further Your kingdom. Please enable me to
open my hands willingly in service.

True Love Means Sacrifice

*They spat on Him, and took the reed and began to
beat Him on the head. After they had mocked Him,
they took the scarlet robe off Him and put His own
garments back on Him, and led Him
away to crucify Him.*

MATTHEW 27:30–31

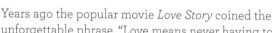

Years ago the popular movie *Love Story* coined the
unforgettable phrase, "Love means never having to say
you're sorry." What a fallacy, and more is the pity for those
who bought into this lie!

For love demands that we always say we're sorry.
How else can relationships be restored? Those two words,
"I'm sorry," have the power to keep families and churches
together.

To admit fallibility is to make a sacrifice. To have done
nothing wrong and to offer the ultimate sacrifice is an act
possible only for God's Son. Jesus' offering of His body at
Calvary gave eternal life to all who believe in Him.

Is there someone from whom you are estranged who is
waiting to hear those two little words? Say you're sorry.

*Lord, You sacrificed all You had to provide my eternal
salvation. Help me today to express true
sorrow for my sins.*

Offerings to the Lord

*"Speak to the sons of Israel and say to them,
'When any man of you brings an offering to the LORD,
you shall bring your offering of animals
from the herd or the flock.'"*

LEVITICUS 1:2

God communicated His Word and His desire for proper worship through His chosen leaders. These spokesmen then communicated His message to His chosen people. Before the coming of the Holy Spirit at Pentecost, this chain of command was vital so that God's flock was not misled.

God required proper and orderly worship. Only an unblemished male animal could be used as the burnt offering. Down through the ages men and women were to make a connection between this sacrifice and the one Christ would willingly make on Calvary's cross.

There have not been any animal sacrifices since the temple in Jerusalem was destroyed in AD 70. Since Christ made His atoning sacrifice on the cross, our sins are forgiven based on His shed blood.

Lord, how grateful I am for Jesus, Your unblemished Lamb. Might I willingly become a living sacrifice through service to You as I take the Gospel to this needy world.

A Woman of Folly

*The woman of folly is boisterous, she is naive
and knows nothing. She sits at the doorway of her house,
on a seat by the high places of the city, calling to those
who pass by, who are making their paths straight:
"Whoever is naive, let him turn in here," and to him
who lacks understanding she says, "Stolen water
is sweet; and bread eaten in secret is pleasant."*

PROVERBS 9:13–17

This woman is not content to wreak havoc on her own life,
but she entices those who wanted to go the right way to
join her on this road to nowhere. The passage describes
her as "naive," because surely if she'd known better she'd
have chosen more wisely.

Have you ever felt like this woman? Did you start out
with endless options and then begin purchasing tickets to
oblivion? With Christ it's not too late to cash in that pass
to nowhere. With Christ your life will have direction.

*Lord, please provide me with a true picture of myself.
Guide me to the place You envision for me.*

To Touch Jesus' Cloak

A woman who had had a hemorrhage for twelve years, and had endured much at the hands of many physicians. . .after hearing about Jesus, she came up in the crowd behind Him and touched His cloak. For she thought, "If I just touch His garments, I will get well."

MARK 5:25–28

The wonder is that this woman could survive for twelve long years. In one last-ditch effort, she reaches out to touch the garment of Jesus as He passes by. Somehow she knows that His very holiness can heal her physically.

"Immediately Jesus, perceiving in Himself that the power proceeding from Him had gone forth, turned around in the crowd and said, 'Who touched My garments?' " (Mark 5:30).

"But the woman fearing and trembling, aware of what had happened to her, came and fell down before Him and told Him the whole truth" (5:33). She's been miraculously healed and now she demonstrates her faith by worshipping at Jesus' feet. Does your faith shine through even in small gestures?

Lord, You heal me when I come to You by renewing my spirit and deepening my faith. I worship Your majesty and power.

The Lord's Diet Plan

"Speak to the sons of Israel, saying, 'These are the creatures which you may eat from all the animals that are on the earth. Whatever divides a hoof, thus making split hoofs, and chews the cud, among the animals, that you may eat.'"

LEVITICUS 11:2-3

Moses was chosen by God to deliver dietary restrictions to the Israelites. The one meat you probably already know about is pork. God didn't even want the Israelites to touch it. He told Moses that although it has "a divided hoof, [it] does not chew the cud; it is unclean for you" (Leviticus 11:7 NIV).

Unlike the cow, the pig doesn't take time to ruminate. So what in the world does this have to do with anything?

In those days prior to refrigeration and pasteurization, if the Israelites hadn't obeyed God's dietary laws, most if not all of them would have died from bacterial infections, food poisoning, and so on. God was preserving a nation from which the Messiah would be born.

Lord, Your call to obedience may not always make sense, but help me remember that You have a reason.

U-Hauls Don't Follow Hearses

*"Lord, make me to know my end and what is the extent
of my days; let me know how transient I am."*

PSALM 39:4

As Christians we know that no human possesses the
ability to access knowledge of future events. Omniscience
belongs to God alone.

God wants us to trust Him for our future. To know our
life span would affect us every day of our life. So, God has
guarded this secret as a great favor to us.

In a church we used to attend, the pastor was famous
for his story about the man who wanted to have a U-Haul
following the hearse to his funeral. None of us will take
the fruits of our labor with us to our eternal destination.
Instead, we should concern ourselves with where that final
stop will be.

To worry about the future is to be uncertain of your
eternity.

*Lord, it's so easy to get caught up in the glitter of gold.
Give me a daily glimpse of heaven, my real home.*

The Wise of Heart

*The wise of heart will receive commands, but a babbling
fool will be ruined. He who walks in integrity walks securely,
but he who perverts his ways will be found out.*

PROVERBS 10:8–9

For years James Dobson, president of Focus on the Family, has warned parents about the pitfalls ahead for their strong-willed children. Personally, we raised our three kids with one hand on the radio and the other on the Bible. Dr. Dobson's radio ministry has given us hope and kept us sane.

My repeated prayer for all our children was this: "Lord, protect them and surround them with Your angels. And if they're disobedient, let them be found out."

Our kids were convinced that I had spies stationed all over the city. No matter what they did, I knew about it within hours. And I can assure you, it was a direct result of this prayer.

Is there a young person in your life who needs your prayers today?

*Lord, help us to stress honesty, obedience,
and the truth of Your Word to our kids and to shower
them with unconditional love so that they can grow
to maturity in a secure emotional place.*

Jesus Drives Out a Demon

Jesus left that place and went to the vicinity of Tyre.
He entered a house and did not want anyone to know it;
yet he could not keep his presence secret. In fact, as soon as
she heard about him, a woman whose little daughter was
possessed by an impure spirit came and fell at his feet.

MARK 7:24–25 NIV

Shocking headlines assault us almost daily, relating the horrors children have inflicted upon other children. Even during the time of Christ, diabolic forces knew no age barriers.

A Gentile woman of Syrophoenician heritage sought out Jesus. A desperate woman, she recognized that her little daughter was demon possessed.

She not only displayed faith in His ability to heal, but also believed that she had the right to ask Him for assistance. Jesus came to bring the Good News to the Jews first. But this woman, a Gentile, said she needed Jesus' touch, too. And He responded to her faith. Ask Jesus to touch your life this day.

Lord, You are Messiah to all, Jews and Gentiles,
and I know You will never turn me away. In this I rejoice!

Commandments or Suggestions?

"'I am the LORD who sanctifies you. . . . You are therefore to keep all My statutes and all My ordinances and do them, so that the land to which I am bringing you to live will not spew you out.'"

LEVITICUS 20:8, 22

When God gave His laws to Moses, He expected them to be observed.

But how could sinful men ever comply consistently with these laws? Therefore, throughout Old Testament history, humanity was to look forward in time and trust God for the coming Messiah; His death would finally cleanse them from their sin. Abraham believed this and passed the "promise" on to his descendants. Isaac then brought this seed of expectation to Jacob. And on and on the word of the Lord progressed.

However, so did man's sin. Our hope lies in the fact that Jesus Christ has paid the penalty for all our sin. And if we confess our sins to Him, then He is faithful and just to forgive us (1 John 1:9).

Lord, having a relationship with You is the only way we can keep Your commands. Help us to relinquish our wills to You.

Jesus Is Transfigured

Jesus took with Him Peter and James and John. . . . And He was transfigured before them; and His garments became radiant and exceedingly white, as no launderer on earth can whiten them. Elijah appeared to them along with Moses; and they were talking with Jesus.

MARK 9:2-4

We can't even imagine what glory these disciples beheld. Their human eyes were allowed to view Jesus virtually transformed into a supernatural form.

The Greek word for this phenomenon of transfiguration is *metamorphoó*, from which we derive our word *metamorphosis*. Christ performs the miracle of metamorphosis in us when we come to believe in Him as Lord and Savior. He transforms us, quickening our spirits so that we are destined to spend eternity with God in heaven. It's a change on the inside that is displayed on the outside—for the unbelieving world to see.

Lord, transform me today, by Your almighty power, into a bold witness of Your Gospel message.

In Memory of the Righteous

*The memory of the righteous is blessed,
but the name of the wicked will rot.*

PROVERBS 10:7

Not long ago I attended the funeral of the mother of one of my husband's coworkers.

Warmth, love, and appreciation greeted my husband and me from the moment we set foot in the chapel, which overflowed with guests. This large family had assembled to provide a magnificent send-off for their precious "Nanay." Amid the battles of World War II, she was widowed at twenty-seven and left with three small children. Yet those difficult days of grief and hardship became her stepping-stones to faith in Christ. Later she remarried and was blessed with five more children.

This woman had lost so much. And yet, blessed with true wisdom, she turned to the Lord for solace and found in Him the foundation on which to build her life. To leave a rich legacy of love, one must be dearly acquainted with the Author of love, our heavenly Father.

Lord, I am blessed by the memory of righteous women. Help me to live in such a worthy manner, that I might be remembered for following after You all my days.

Jesus Prophesies His Death

*Those who followed were fearful. And again He took
the twelve aside and began to tell them what was going
to happen to Him, saying, "Behold, we are going up to
Jerusalem, and the Son of Man will be delivered to the
chief priests and the scribes; and they will condemn Him
to death, and will hand Him over to the Gentiles.
They will mock Him and spit on Him, and scourge Him
and kill Him, and three days later He will rise again."*

MARK 10:32-34

Christ's disciples couldn't cope with the thought of His
leaving and therefore became fearful. Jesus encouraged
them with the hope of His resurrection.

And when He had risen from the dead, "He opened
their minds to understand the Scriptures, and He said to
them, 'Thus it is written, that the Christ would suffer and
rise again from the dead the third day, and that repentance
for the forgiveness of sins would be proclaimed in His
name to all the nations, beginning from Jerusalem. You are
witnesses of these things'" (Luke 24:45–48).

*Lord, when grief overwhelms us, let us remember Your
death provides our hope of eternal life.*

God Orders a Census

*"Take a census of all the congregation of the sons of Israel,
by their families, by their fathers' households, according to
the number of names, every male, head by head from twenty
years old and upward, whoever is able to go out to war in
Israel, you and Aaron shall number them by their armies.
With you, moreover, there shall be a man of each tribe,
each one head of his father's household."*

NUMBERS 1:2–4

The Israelites, who were constantly at odds with the
Gentile nations surrounding them, needed to know the
strength of their army. So God showed Moses a systematic
way to determine this number.

Notice that men were conscripted to serve Israel's
army from the time they were twenty years old until they
were no longer able to serve. In doing so, they would be
preserving their nation clear into the time in history when
the Messiah would finally be born.

*Lord, with You everything has a plan.
In a world that is filled with nebulous thinking,
I can rely on Your consistency.*

By Whose Authority Did Jesus Act?

The chief priests and the scribes and the elders came to Him, and began saying to Him, "By what authority are You doing these things, or who gave You this authority to do these things?" And Jesus said to them, "I will ask you one question, and you answer Me, and then I will tell you by what authority I do these things. Was the baptism of John from heaven, or from men? Answer Me."

MARK 11:27-30

The Pharisees, the Jewish religious leaders, made sure the Mosaic laws were adhered to. They read the laws day and night, probably looking for ones that had been broken. The scribes were given the task of recording every "jot and tittle" of the Word of God. Both groups not only knew the law but also understood what the Messiah would do when He came.

Jesus Christ cannot be fooled. He knew the hearts of the Pharisees and scribes, and He knows your heart, too.

Jesus, You spoke plainly about who You are. Help me hear.

Never Take a Drink?

*Again the LORD spoke to Moses, saying, "Speak to the sons
of Israel and say to them, 'When a man or woman makes
a special vow, the vow of a Nazirite, to dedicate himself to
the LORD, he shall abstain from wine and strong drink.' "*

NUMBERS 6:1–3

When I became a Christian at age twenty-nine, drinking
was the first thing to go out of my life. Along with all
the warnings against strong drink that I read in the
Bible, there was family history. My father had been an
alcoholic.

After making a decision to follow Christ, I recognized
the risk of potentially harming the young children my
husband and I were raising. Like a Nazarite submitting to
his vow, I refused to provide a breeding ground in which
this substance might interfere with the plans God desired
for my life and future. And the Lord has remained faithful
to provide all the inspiration I need.

*Whatever is preventing me from seeing only You,
Lord, provide the strength I require to set it aside.*

Some Will Be Singing

*And they sang the song of Moses, the bond-servant of God,
and the song of the Lamb, saying, "Great and marvelous
are Your works, O Lord God, the Almighty; righteous
and true are Your ways, King of the nations!"*
REVELATION 15:3

Those who are victorious over the adversities of the last
days on earth will have much to celebrate. This victorious
number will include many Jews who come to believe in
Christ as their Messiah. And in true Israelite fashion, they
will express their jubilation in song, just as King David
did. For the covenant God made with His people stands
for all time: "He has sent redemption to His people; He
has ordained His covenant forever; holy and awesome
is His name. The fear of the LORD is the beginning of
wisdom; a good understanding have all those who do
His commandments; His praise endures forever" (Psalm
111:9–11).

*Lord, You alone are worthy of our worship. I praise you
with all my heart and look forward to the day
when I will worship You in heaven.*

Walking in the Light of God's Goodness

The fear of the LORD prolongs life, but the years of the wicked will be shortened. The hope of the righteous is gladness, but the expectation of the wicked perishes. The way of the LORD is a stronghold to the upright.

PROVERBS 10:27-29

Instead of being a cause of terror in our hearts, the phrase "fear of the Lord" means to reverence and honor Him as God. For He alone is God, righteous and wise enough to intervene and effect positive changes in our lives. Instilling this truth in our children enables them to know the ways of the Lord.

God's very nature is goodness. Therefore, everything that stems from Him reflects His character. This knowledge should cause hope to flood our lives. Unshaken by the winds of change, we can stand firm in the face of any kind of adversity, like a boat anchored to its strong moorings.

Lord, show us how to raise children who reflect the goodness of Your character!

Sinners from Birth

Behold, I was brought forth in iniquity,
and in sin my mother conceived me.

PSALM 51:5

You need to get straight in this passage what God's Word is *not* saying. The union of man and woman, within the bounds of marriage, is absolutely God's design and purpose. These verses are not alluding to the act of love that produces a child. Rather, David is stating that each of us is born with the same sin nature as Adam.

David spoke from the depths of his guilty, broken heart. He had viewed the lovely Bathsheba as she prepared to bathe on her rooftop. Hypnotized by her beauty, he "took her to bed." And when she became pregnant, he plotted a murderous solution that would send her husband, Uriah, to the front lines of battle.

Admitting our own sinful state is the first step toward a more sincere Christian walk. And acknowledging the sin in our children makes us more effective Christian parents.

David didn't acknowledge his sin until You sent Nathan the prophet to convict his soul. What will it take for me, Lord?

Sibling Rivalry

*Then the LORD. . .called Aaron and Miriam. . . . He said,
"Hear now My words: If there is a prophet among you,
I, the LORD, shall make Myself known to him in a vision.
I shall speak with him in a dream. Not so, with My
servant Moses, he is faithful in all My household."*

NUMBERS 12:5–7

God speaks face-to-face with Moses, and Aaron and
Miriam become jealous. So God comes down in a pillar of
cloud. When the cloud is withdrawn from over the Tent of
Meeting, Miriam's skin has become leprous.

God leaves Miriam to mull over her rebellious and
questioning spirit for seven days. And then the Lord
graciously heals her, at the request of Moses.

How could she even think of asking God to explain
Himself? But don't we all do the same thing when the
going gets rough? How about, "If there's a God, then why
is there so much suffering?"

The power to make a choice between good and evil is
a gift from God. What we do with the gift is up to us.

*Lord, please help me understand that Your
actions are always in my best interest.*

When Fear Paralyzes

A young man was following Him, wearing nothing but a linen sheet over his naked body; and they seized him. But he pulled free of the linen sheet and escaped naked. They led Jesus away to the high priest; and all the chief priests and the elders and the scribes gathered together.

MARK 14:51-53

Suddenly you awake at one in the morning to the sound of the doorknob being turned, followed by the sound of creaking boards. Your heart leaps into your throat. What do you do?

When John Mark, the writer of this Gospel, learned that Jesus had been captured by the Roman guards and a trial was pending, he grabbed the sheet off his bed and ran to observe the events himself.

We know John Mark escaped the threatening situation. Yet Jesus Christ remained in the eye of the storm, well aware of the situation yet in perfect sync with the Father. When fear paralyzes, help is only a prayer away.

Lord, I believe in all that You are, both God and Man.

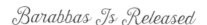

Barabbas Is Released

Pilate answered them, saying, "Do you want me to release for you the King of the Jews?"... But the chief priests stirred up the crowd to ask him to release Barabbas for them instead.

MARK 15:9, 11

Why did the chief priests incite the people to choose Barabbas?

The priests were but players in the great drama prophesied hundreds of years earlier in the Old Testament. Jesus Christ would be sentenced to death by Pilate even though Pilate found Him without guilt. Jesus Christ must die for the sins of humankind.

Today we know the truth. And we can share, without fear, without guilt, the kingship of Jesus Christ.

What would I have shouted if I had been part of that crowd? And what affirmation do I give You today, Lord?

Joseph of Arimathea

Joseph of Arimathea came, a prominent member of the Council, who himself was waiting for the kingdom of God; and he gathered up courage and went in before Pilate, and asked for the body of Jesus.

MARK 15:43

Today's scripture reading, along with parallel passages from the other three Gospels, discloses that Joseph of Arimathea had become "a secret disciple of Christ." Yet now, accompanied by Nicodemus, another member of the ruling council of religious leaders, Joseph of Arimathea displayed an incredible boldness of character. For Joseph requested Christ's body for burial; then he and Nicodemus lovingly prepared their Lord for His burial.

Christ nurtured the faith of both these men, safely reserving them for His divine purpose within the realm of authority in which He had placed them. They were needed for just such a time, because down through the ages to come, the faith of other believers would hinge on the fact that Christ really died and really was resurrected.

Lord, the tomb is empty, and the grave clothes left behind signify for all time that You have risen from the dead. And because You live, we can face whatever tomorrow brings!

Where Do You Take Refuge?

When I am afraid, I will put my trust in You. In God,
whose word I praise, in God I have put my trust; I shall
not be afraid. What can mere man do to me?

PSALM 56:3-4

David wrote this psalm when the Philistines had seized him in Gath. These Philistines had been enemies of the Israelites for a long time. At one point they'd even stolen the ark of the covenant! They'd probably never forgiven David for killing their giant, Goliath. I wonder if David reflected during his present predicament, remembering the time in his youth when he'd faced that giant with only five smooth stones and a sling. He had called upon his God to deliver him, and the Lord had prevailed (1 Samuel 17:37–50).

Where do you go for refuge? I run to the arms of my loving Father, just as David did in his own crisis. And He always comes through.

O Lord, You alone are my refuge and strength.
Help me to come to You first in a crisis.

John the Baptist Is Born

They were both righteous in the sight of God,
walking blamelessly in all the commandments
and requirements of the Lord. But they had no child,
because Elizabeth was barren, and they
were both advanced in years.

LUKE 1:6-7

Zacharias could be found day after day in the temple, obediently "performing his priestly service before God" (Luke 1:8).

One day, as he offered incense before the altar, an angel of the Lord appeared and said, "Do not be afraid, Zacharias, for your petition has been heard, and your wife Elizabeth will bear you a son, and you will give him the name John" (1:13).

Now Zacharias asks, "How will I know this for certain?" (1:18). Fulfillment of that promise still looked impossible to him.

So poor Zacharias was struck dumb. Elizabeth did become pregnant, just as the angel had said. And during her sixth month, her cousin Mary came to tell her that she, too, was carrying a child. One day their sons would meet by the Jordan River. This was God's perfect plan, the fulfillment of His promises.

Lord, restore my hope in You today.

God's Deterrent to Sin

So Israel joined themselves to Baal of Peor, and the
LORD was angry against Israel. The LORD said to Moses,
"Take all the leaders of the people and execute them
in broad daylight before the LORD, so that the fierce
anger of the LORD may turn away from Israel."

NUMBERS 25:3-4

God had watched over Israel in war and in peace. He
had delivered them safely to a land flowing with milk
and honey; He had promised them a Messiah. But if the
Israelites continued to kill their children by sacrificing
them to Baal, the line to Christ would be wiped out before
He ever arrived on the scene.

God was forced to purge from Israel those who chose
to lead others astray.

If you're a parent, you probably devote much time and
energy to keeping your children from getting involved in
things that would harm them. In the same way, God, our
loving Parent, must pull in the reins when we drift too far
from His truth.

Lord, shine Your beacon of truth on those who are in
leadership, that they may never lead others astray.

Anna the Prophetess

*And there was a prophetess, Anna the daughter of
Phanuel, of the tribe of Asher.... She never left the temple,
serving night and day with fastings and prayers.
At that very moment she came up and began giving
thanks to God, and continued to speak of Him to all those
who were looking for the redemption of Jerusalem.*

LUKE 2:36–38

Anna had faithfully served in the temple her entire life.
And despite her advanced age, she remained there even
after others had gone home for the evening. She was a
prophetess; she foretold the truths of God to the people.
No wonder He used her life.

God had promised Anna that she would see the
Messiah before she died. She waited eighty-four years,
biding her time in service to the Lord. And He kept His
word. Let us strive to follow Anna's prayerful example, and
we, too, will be blessed by God.

*Lord, call my heart to faithfulness and prayer.
May I serve as an example to encourage others.*

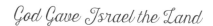

God Gave Israel the Land

*Then the LORD spoke to Moses, saying, "Among these the
land shall be divided for an inheritance according to the
number of names. . . . Each shall be given their inheritance
according to those who were numbered of them.
But the land shall be divided by lot. They shall receive
their inheritance according to the names
of the tribes of their fathers."*

NUMBERS 26:52–55

God picked for Himself a people, the Jews. And He
blessed them with this land as an inheritance. It's not
too late for Israel's enemies to repent. Yet with each new
wave of terrorism and attacks against Israel, we know that
nothing short of divine intervention will free the Jews from
annihilation.

Christ is coming back as the ultimate Judge and
Rescuer of Israel. The time is now to be sure of our
commitment to Jesus Christ and that of our loved ones.

*Lord, I pray that men and women repent while there is yet
time. I look forward to the establishment of
Your perfect kingdom.*

One Calling in the Desert

The word of God came to John, the son of Zacharias,
in the wilderness. And he came into all the district
around the Jordan, preaching a baptism of
repentance for forgiveness of sins.

As John came into the district around the Jordan River,
the religious leaders used their influence to attempt to
dissuade the people from the truth about the Messiah.
John called them a "brood of vipers" (Luke 3:7). And
then he added, "Therefore bear fruits in keeping with
repentance, and do not begin to say to yourselves, 'We
have Abraham for our father,' for I say to you that from
these stones God is able to raise up children to Abraham"
(3:8).

The religious leaders called themselves Abraham's
children. Yet being Abraham's children required that they
display faith.

John's exhortations were aimed at the "wilderness of
men's souls." How many churchgoers do you know who
claim the faith yet exist in a wasteland of sin?

Lord, You sent John to proclaim Your beloved Son.
Help me to proclaim Your Word and
love to anyone, anywhere.

A Refuge from Our Despair

Hear my cry, O God; give heed to my prayer. From the end of
the earth I call to You when my heart is faint; lead me to the
rock that is higher than I. For You have been a refuge for me,
a tower of strength against the enemy. Let me dwell in Your
tent forever; let me take refuge in the shelter of Your wings.

PSALM 61:1-4

King David, writer of this psalm, composed it as a song,
acknowledging God as his rock. Although David's trials
may differ from yours, you, too, can use strong coping
mechanisms.

First, David acknowledged that God remained all-
powerful, despite life circumstances. And second, David
looked back at God's past rescues. "O my God, my soul is
in despair within me; therefore I remember You from the
land of the Jordan and the peaks of Hermon, from Mount
Mizar" (Psalm 42:6).

Lord, I search for a way through the torrents of despair.
How precious is the knowledge that You hear and care.

Why Mary and Joseph Married

"Every daughter who comes into possession of an inheritance of any tribe of the sons of Israel shall be wife to one of the family of the tribe of her father, so that the sons of Israel each may possess the inheritance of his fathers."

NUMBERS 36:8

The Gospels of Matthew and Luke present Christ's genealogy. Although Joseph was not Christ's father, he belonged to the tribe of Judah, just as Mary did. Both came from a godly line.

Mary had led a life of purity, revering God's Word and looking forward to the Savior whom God had promised. When God sent an angel to announce His plan, Mary responded in obedience.

Mary and Joseph married because they loved each other, but more importantly, both of them loved God and desired to be a part of His purpose for humankind. And within this environment of submission, Israel's inheritance—the Savior—remained secure.

Lord, we know that Joseph loved Mary and both were chosen by You. Yet they also obeyed You in their choice of a life partner.

Jesus Is Tempted by Satan

And the devil said to Him, "If You are the Son of God,
tell this stone to become bread." And Jesus answered him,
"It is written, 'MAN SHALL NOT LIVE ON BREAD ALONE.' "

LUKE 4:3-4

Have you ever found yourself so tempted to sin that you ached all the way to your soul? Christ understands that pull toward evil.

Satan wasn't just present in the wilderness to "bug" the Lord Jesus Christ. This was a full-on frontal attack. And the stakes were high. For if Christ succumbed to Satan's snare, He would be ineligible to make that perfect sacrifice on the cross as the Lamb of God without blemish.

Lord, I thank You for Your Son's
perfect victory over Satan.

Matthew the Tax Collector

After that He went out and noticed a tax collector
named Levi sitting in the tax booth, and He said to him,
"Follow Me." And he left everything behind, and got up and
began to follow Him. And Levi gave a big reception for Him
in his house; and there was a great crowd of tax collectors
and other people who were reclining at the table with them.

LUKE 5:27–29

Oh no, not the dreaded tax man! Yet Levi responded to Christ's invitation to follow Him. Christ changed his name from Levi to Matthew, which means "gift of God." Whatever flaws Matthew possessed prior to this time no longer mattered.

Because of his record-keeping skills and attention to detail, Matthew made an excellent and meticulous Gospel writer. He'd been regenerated by Christ, and the Lord could use his talents to further the kingdom.

Lord, after all these years, attitudes remain the same
about tax collectors. Please help me to see them as
You saw Matthew, as people who know
You or are in need of a Savior.

Moses Appoints Judges

"The Lord your God has multiplied you, and behold,
you are this day as the stars of heaven in number.
May the Lord, the God of your fathers, increase
you a thousand-fold more than you are and
bless you, just as He has promised you!"

DEUTERONOMY 1:10–11

The Israelites were two million strong when they left Egypt, and now in "the fortieth year, on the first day of the eleventh month" (Deuteronomy 1:3), Moses proclaimed to them what the Lord had commanded.

The people had been in this same place forty years earlier, but the Israelites disobeyed God by refusing to fight for the land and to trust God for the victory.

Therefore, God announced that this entire generation of rebellious people—with two exceptions, Caleb and Joshua—would not see the Promised Land. Even Moses, who had displayed a lack of faith, would not set foot there. God demands trust from His people and His spiritual leaders.

Do you trust God for everything?

Dear heavenly Father, let my trust in You never
waver. Give me wisdom and courage for this day.

The Eternal Gospel

"Fear God, and give Him glory, because the hour of His judgment has come; worship Him who made the heaven and the earth and sea and springs of waters."

REVELATION 14:7

Following the resurrection, Jesus prepared to leave this earth and return to heaven. Before going, He delivered a message to His disciples and charged them with a mission: "Go therefore and make disciples of all the nations, baptizing them in the name of the Father and the Son and the Holy Spirit, teaching them to observe all that I commanded you; and lo, I am with you always, even to the end of the age" (Matthew 28:19–20).

This great commission is extended to all who choose to believe in Christ.

Lord, while there is still time, please provide imaginative ways in which we can speak forth Your Word of Truth to all those whom we love. We are grateful that You will never leave us or forsake us (Hebrews 13:5).

Our Triune God

"Hear, O Israel! The LORD is our God, the LORD is one!"
DEUTERONOMY 6:4

Shema Yisroel Adonai Elohenu Adonai Echad is Hebrew for "Hear, O Israel! The LORD our God is one LORD." The three distinct personalities that comprise the Trinity are all equal within the Godhead: Father, Son, and Holy Spirit. But the word "one" here should be interpreted as in a marriage context when the "two become one."

Genesis 1:1 states, "In the beginning God created the heavens and the earth." The Hebrew word for God here is *Elohim*, a masculine plural noun. When God speaks of Himself, the plural pronoun is used: "Then God [*Elohim*] said, 'Let Us make man in Our image, according to Our likeness' " (Genesis 1:26). All three persons of the Trinity were present.

Only God could have omnisciently conceived of the Trinity. God has always been and will forever be.

Lord, I rejoice in my wonderful Savior, the Father who sent Him, and the Holy Spirit who gives me insight to understand scripture.

Paul's Ministry Comes to a Close

Paul, an apostle of Christ Jesus by the will of God,
according to the promise of life in Christ Jesus,
to Timothy, my beloved son.... I constantly remember
you in my prayers night and day, longing to see you,
even as I recall your tears, so that I may be filled with joy.
For I am mindful of the sincere faith within you,
which first dwelt in your grandmother Lois
and your mother Eunice, and I am sure
that it is in you as well.

2 TIMOTHY 1:1–5

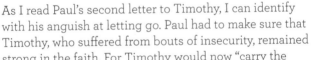

As I read Paul's second letter to Timothy, I can identify with his anguish at letting go. Paul had to make sure that Timothy, who suffered from bouts of insecurity, remained strong in the faith. For Timothy would now "carry the torch of faith" and continue bringing the Gospel to all who would listen.

Paul praises Timothy, reminding him of the heritage of belief passed down to him from his mother, Eunice, and grandmother, Lois. And Paul, the ever-present spiritual mentor, expresses his love by referring to Timothy as "my beloved son."

Use me, Lord, to do Your will.

A Call to Holiness

"When you enter the land which the LORD your God
gives you, you shall not learn to imitate the
detestable things of those nations."

DEUTERONOMY 18:9

Our two sons became immediately fascinated with the
role-playing game Dungeons and Dragons. While our
older son got a part-time job, which severely limited his
free time, his younger brother went deeper and deeper into
this seductive game.

About the same time, our church encouraged adults
and high schoolers to sign up for the seminar "Basic Youth
Conflicts." By the time the concluding all-day Saturday
session rolled around, each one of us had been convicted
by the Holy Spirit concerning our own "pet sins." All the
way home that last evening, our younger son spoke about
how the game had usurped the time he used to spend with
the Lord.

We watched as he pulled out a metal trash can and
burned every one of the game's expensive books. From that
moment Jeff never looked back.

Is God receiving all the glory in your life?

Lord, You know better than I what things will
draw my time and attention away from You.
Give me the courage to obey You.

Moses Is in Glory

*And behold, two men were talking with Him;
and they were Moses and Elijah, who, appearing in glory,
were speaking of His departure which He was
about to accomplish at Jerusalem.*

LUKE 9:30–31

In case you've been feeling sorry for Moses who never got to enter the Promised Land, just look at what God had in store for him. These verses tell us that Moses and Elijah appeared in glory. But what does that really mean?

We are not now what we will become. For whether we die or are taken up by what is referred to as the Rapture, the Lord will someday allow this "earth suit" of ours to fall away and issue us our "eternity suit."

In spite of your life, are you assured of your salvation?

*Oh Lord, I am so grateful that my place with
You is already reserved!*

A Rock of Refuge

For You are my rock and my fortress.
PSALM 71:3

For several months before I attended my first writers' conference in Southern California, I worked feverishly compiling a manuscript for a book. However, when an editor at the conference looked it over, he told me that it needed work. Being new to the field of writing, I was devastated by his remarks.

I sought solace upon a large rock situated beside a small lake. Tears of disappointment streaked down my cheeks and as others approached I began walking. I happened to encounter a bronze plaque that stated that the well-known evangelist Billy Graham had also found peace in this place.

As the sun warmed that beautiful, tranquil setting, I considered another psalm about the Rock. "Be to me a rock of strength, a stronghold to save me. For You are my rock and my fortress; for Your name's sake You will lead me and guide me" (Psalm 31:2–3).

Over fifty times in scripture the word *rock* is used in reference to God. He is steadfast, immovable, and unchangeable.

Lord, You remain that Rock on which my faith stands firm.

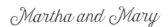

Martha and Mary

A woman named Martha welcomed Him into her home.
She had a sister called Mary, who was seated at the Lord's
feet, listening to His word. But Martha was distracted with
all her preparations; and she came up to Him and said,
"Lord, do You not care that my sister has left me to do
all the serving alone? Then tell her to help me."

LUKE 10:38-40

Martha, ever the perfect hostess, was left to do all the work. It didn't seem fair. However, what Martha really desired was a release from her compulsive neatness. And that's when the Lord presented her with a process for "chilling out."

Who knew better than Christ how to put the pressures of life into perspective? He had only three years in which to establish His ministry, train up His disciples, and present the Gospel. Yet we see no record of Him hurrying others or running at a frantic pace.

Have you taken time to get to know your Lord? Perhaps your life, like Martha's, is missing the best part.

Lord, I pray for peace today from my busy
schedule so I may learn at Your knee.

The Lord of Parables

Listen, O my people, to my instruction; incline your ears to
the words of my mouth. I will open my mouth in a parable;
I will utter dark sayings of old, which we have heard
and known, and our fathers have told us.

PSALM 78:1-3

Christ did not dabble in nonsense. But sometimes Jesus
offered His perfect insight in parables, or through stories
with hidden meanings. "To you it has been granted to
know the mysteries of the kingdom of God, but to the
rest it is in parables, that SEEING THEY MAY NOT SEE, AND
HEARING THEY MAY NOT UNDERSTAND" (Luke 8:10).

Jesus had just shared with them the parable about
the sower and the seed. He knew that those whose hearts
were open and receptive to Him would understand its
meaning. On the other hand, those whose hearts held only
antagonism, jealousy, and self-righteousness would not
understand even if He spoke plainly.

Is your heart ready to listen to Jesus?

When You examine the content of my heart, Lord,
which type of soil have I prepared for Your Word?

Joshua Is Chosen

"Be strong and courageous, for you shall go with this people into the land which the LORD has sworn to their fathers to give them, and you shall give it to them as an inheritance."
DEUTERONOMY 31:7

God did not allow those who taunted Moses to challenge the authority of his successor. Moses, who is preparing to die, names Joshua as his successor. Right there, in the presence of all Israel, Moses admonishes Joshua to "be strong and courageous." God chose Joshua because he had faithfully served Moses throughout all their years in the wilderness.

With his last bit of energy, Moses recited the words of the song God had given to him (Deuteronomy 32:1–2 NIV). "Listen, you heavens, and I will speak; hear, you earth, the words of my mouth. Let my teaching fall like rain and my words descend like dew, like showers on new grass, like abundant rain on tender plants."—and then it continues for forty-one more verses. Please take time to read it all.

Lord, I forget sometimes that those in leadership are chosen by You. And with responsibility comes accountability.

Welcoming Other Believers

The elder to the beloved Gaius, whom I love in truth. . . . Beloved, you are acting faithfully in whatever you accomplish for the brethren, and especially when they are strangers.

3 JOHN 1:1, 5

Gaius, a strong and cordial believer, was dearly loved by the apostle John. We see in today's scripture that John refers to him as "beloved." Gaius extended a hand of loving fellowship to all who came to worship.

But it was the truth to which Gaius was a witness that had molded this extraordinary life, one centered on obedience to God. Gaius provided genuine hospitality. And evidently this included opening his own home, heart, and pocketbook to others so that the Word of God might go forth.

If only we all might have such pure motives for assisting others—that they might receive God's Word and see His love flowing all around them.

Father, sometimes my church is filled with people who may only "press the flesh with the faithful" once or twice a year. May I give these inquiring minds a warm reception.

Order in Our Prayers

First of all, then, I urge that entreaties and prayers,
petitions and thanksgivings, be made on behalf of all men,
for kings and all who are in authority, so that we may lead
a tranquil and quiet life in all godliness and dignity.
This is good and acceptable in the sight of God our
Savior, who desires all men to be saved and to
come to the knowledge of the truth.

1 TIMOTHY 2:1–4

The demands of this world, and the pace at which our technology is racing, can sometimes overwhelm us, causing feelings of panic, powerlessness, and even paranoia. Is there a solution that brings life back into perspective? Yes. And God calls it prayer.

Prayer isn't some mystical entity to be attained by a few saintly little ladies in the church. Instead, it is an act of worship on the part of the created toward the Creator. Prayer is simply "talking to God" about everything that affects our lives.

Spirit of God, fall afresh on me that I might lift
my voice in petition to You.

The God of Our Salvation

Help us, O God of our salvation, for the glory of Your name;
and deliver us and forgive our sins for Your name's sake.
Why should the nations say, "Where is their God?"
Let there be known among the nations in our sight,
vengeance for the blood of Your servants
which has been shed.

PSALM 79:9–10

God swore to Israel that He loved them. Now David calls upon the Lord to forgive the people, knowing full well that their present troubles directly correspond to their disobedience.

Have you ever cried out to God for deliverance, recognizing that your own circumstances were a direct result of leaving the Lord out of the decision making? We've all been there at one time or another. But God's not surprised. He watched us make this awful choice and then witnessed the harm we did to ourselves and others.

However, David recognized that if he didn't "own his sin" and ask forgiveness from his Lord, there was absolutely no hope for new beginnings.

We thank You that we can come to You as Lord and Messiah. You are truly a God of forgiveness.

Jesus Christ Came in the Flesh

Anyone who goes too far and does not abide in the teaching of Christ, does not have God; the one who abides in the teaching, he has both the Father and the Son. If anyone comes to you and does not bring this teaching, do not receive him into your house, and do not give him a greeting; for the one who gives him a greeting participates in his evil deeds.

2 JOHN 1:9-11

There is no greater evil than to fail to recognize who Jesus Christ is, God in the flesh. God has tried from the beginning of time to build a bridge to humankind. He gave men and women His laws and yet they failed to obey. Then the Lord sent His prophets. But the people refused to listen. And finally, He sent Jesus to show us how to live upon the earth. And instead of responding to His offer of salvation, men nailed Him to a cross.

Lord, strengthen my faith so that I can love those who don't know You, so that I can reveal the true identity of Your Son.

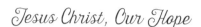

Jesus Christ, Our Hope

To Timothy, my true child in the faith: Grace, mercy and
peace from God the Father and Christ Jesus our Lord.
As I urged you upon my departure for Macedonia,
remain on at Ephesus so that you may instruct certain
men not to teach strange doctrines. . . . But the goal
of our instruction is love from a pure heart and
a good conscience and a sincere faith.

1 TIMOTHY 1:2–3, 5

Paul wrote this letter to encourage Timothy in his own
leadership role, knowing that the worst thing this young
believer could do was to try to emulate Paul instead of
Christ. For Paul held no doubt in his mind concerning
Timothy's call from God. "This command I entrust to
you, Timothy, my son, in accordance with the prophecies
previously made concerning you, that by them you fight
the good fight, keeping faith and a good conscience, which
some have rejected and suffered shipwreck in regard to
their faith" (1 Timothy 1:18–19).

Lord, show me how to use my special gifts.

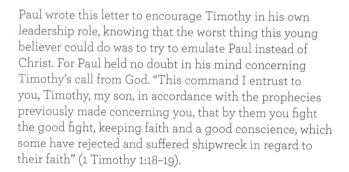

Twelve Stones

---

*"When you come to the edge of the waters of the Jordan,
you shall stand still in the Jordan."*

JOSHUA 3:8

Joshua had gathered the people together, revealing the Lord's words. Then the people left their tents and followed the priests who carried the ark of the covenant. When they reached the banks of the Jordan, the water stopped flowing. . .and the nation of Israel crossed over!

The men of Israel now followed God's command, "Take up for yourselves twelve stones from here out of the middle of the Jordan" (Joshua 4:3). These stones represented each of the tribes of Israel. Piled up high, they produced a visible monument to the miracle God performed.

The forty-thousand-man liberation force, fully equipped for battle, then proceeded to cross the desert plains of Jericho.

As the news spread of God's miracle, so did the level of terror. Jericho was "locked down and secured" behind its gates. But God instructed Israel's warriors to march around the city for six days. No obstacle can prevent God's plan from being realized!

*Lord, please pave my way with stones from You,
stones of dedication, perseverance, and compassion.*

Jesus Alone Is Worthy

*"Stop weeping; behold, the Lion that is from the tribe
of Judah, the Root of David, has overcome so as
to open the book and its seven seals."*

REVELATION 5:5

As the Lamb stood to receive "the book," an awed hush fell
over His celestial audience. He alone was worthy because
He had met God's requirements to redeem the earth. The
prize was His.

The judgments of God comprise the book. These are a
series of progressively worsening catastrophes, deserved
by those who have consistently rejected God, salvation in
Christ, and His Word.

*Lord, I know that Jesus Christ is God in the flesh,
born to die on the cross for my sins. Because of His
sacrifice, I will be able to celebrate forever
with Him in heaven.*

The Father Has Commanded Us to Love

*Grace, mercy and peace will be with us, from God
the Father and from Jesus Christ, the Son
of the Father, in truth and love.*

2 JOHN 1:3

A foundation of any small-group home Bible study should
be the love its members display toward one another. It was
just such a group that John addressed in this letter.

As a church elder, John reminded these believers that
God didn't consider loving one another an option (2 John 1:6).

John shows us the process by which the Word of the
Lord can penetrate our hearts. First, we are to know the
truth (1:1–3), for it is by God's grace that we can love others.

Next, John admonishes us to walk according to His
commandments (1:4–6).

Lastly, we must abide in the truth, who is Christ
(1:7–11).

*Jesus Christ. . .heralded by a star, proclaimed by angels,
announced by the shepherds, and given by the Father to
a world in need of a Savior. Oh, come let us adore Him!*

Living with a View of Heaven

How lovely are Your dwelling places, O LORD of hosts!
My soul longed and even yearned for the courts of the
LORD; my heart and my flesh sing for joy to the living God.

PSALM 84:1-2

King David had an eternal perspective. Israel constantly battled its enemies. How he must have longed for a lasting peace. But he had to settle for that little niche of peace he carved out for himself while pondering what heaven was like, anticipating the day he'd dwell with God. For the God of perfection created for Himself a place of eternal security.

What wonderful knowledge we have that God desires to share this incredible place with His imperfect creatures! Despite our sinful nature, God truly loves us with an eternal affection.

David accepted Your love for him, Lord.
Help me to live in Your will so that my
life is a blessing to You.

True and Lasting Justice

*"In a certain city there was a judge who did not fear
God and did not respect man. There was a widow in that
city, and she kept coming to him, saying, 'Give me legal
protection from my opponent.' For a while he was unwilling;
but afterward he said to himself, 'Even though I do not fear
God nor respect man, yet because this widow bothers
me, I will give her legal protection, otherwise by
continually coming she will wear me out.'"*

LUKE 18:2–5

In New Testament times, whether a case was considered
depended upon the plaintiff's ability to gain the attention
of the judge's attendants. This widow already had three
strikes against her. As a woman, she had no priority
standing in the court. As a widow, she didn't have a
husband to fight for her in these legal proceedings. And
finally, without the funds to pay for assistance, she was
without hope.

If you've been denied justice here on earth, you have a
God who sees all and knows all. Justice will be served!

*Lord, You judge rightly. You will administer
to the guilty the punishment they truly deserve.*

Idols of Their Own Making

Among the gods there is none like you, Lord;
no deeds can compare with yours. . . . For you are
great and do marvelous deeds; you alone are God.

PSALM 86:8, 10 NIV

When men and women refuse to worship the true God, they invariably end up trying to fashion one on their own. The reason is natural: We were all created with a "God-shaped void" inside our souls. The purpose of this void is to draw us to the Lord in commitment.

Satan applies every subversive tactic in his arsenal to dim our understanding of God's attributes. Therefore, it's up to us to find the truth to combat the evil one's lies. At the same time, God is constantly guiding us in our search for knowledge and understanding.

Lord, You've given me an entire Bible to read so that
I might learn of Your love, concern, and compassion.
Develop in me the sensitivity to hear the prompting of
Your Spirit while You guide me toward the truth.

Riding on a Donkey

*"Go into the village ahead of you; there, as you enter,
you will find a colt tied on which no one yet has ever sat;
untie it and bring it here. If anyone asks you, 'Why are you
untying it?' you shall say, 'The Lord has need of it.'"*

LUKE 19:30-31

Jesus came to them riding on a donkey, just as it had been prophesied. But why a donkey? The reason was that He might present Himself to them as their humble servant and King. If He had ridden into Jerusalem on a horse, He would have presented Himself as a warrior, ready for battle. That horse has already been prophesied for the end times (Revelation 19:11).

*Lord, thank You for all the "absolutes" of scripture.
I believe You are exactly who You claim
to be, God Incarnate.*

In the Beginning, Christ

*In the beginning was the Word, and the Word was with God,
and the Word was God. He was in the beginning with God.*

JOHN 1:1–2

An elderly woman once lived next door to us whom
everyone came to call "Aunt Esther." At ninety-one, Esther
had a spunky, conquer-any-obstacle attitude that drew
people to her.

But the church she attended was nothing more than a
cult of false teachers. These teachers presented a new spin
on an old lie, saying Jesus Christ did not exist in the flesh
but was instead spirit.

Aunt Esther would sit and take a dose of the Bible, but
she followed the Truth with a soul-poisoning gulp from
her cult's own book. Over and over I recited the first three
verses of John's Gospel to her. At the age of ninety-three
she suffered a stroke. Knowing her death was imminent,
I lay on the floor next to her bed, praying all through the
night. When she died a day later, she knew Christ as her
Savior.

*Lord, I am so grateful to You for taking all those
who profess Your name to be with You!*

The Wise Woman Builds Her House

The wise woman builds her house, but the foolish tears it down with her own hands. He who walks in his uprightness fears the LORD, but he who is devious in his ways despises Him.

PROVERBS 14:1-2

Every woman must understand God's "building codes" in order to strengthen her own household. The blueprints must be followed. From these, a concrete foundation is laid. Likewise, how can a woman provide guidance within her home unless she first seeks wisdom from the Lord?

Next comes the framing. This skeletal structure furnishes the undergirding and strength to support the home. Prayer is just such sustenance to the family.

Now the insulation is added within the walls. This corresponds to godly friends and church members who provide a cushion to bolster us during the storms of life.

Finally, color-coated stucco and trim put the finishing touches on the exterior of the house. Our family portrays a unique image within our neighborhood. And the love we have for each other reflects the love and worship given to God.

Lord, You are the Master Builder. To stay upright I must follow Your blueprints.

He Dwelt Among Us

*And the Word became flesh, and dwelt among us,
and we saw His glory, glory as of the only begotten
from the Father, full of grace and truth.*

JOHN 1:14

That phrase "dwelt among us" means God took on the form of a human body, leaving the peace, security, and hope of heaven, and came to earth to become a model for men and women.

How do you teach children not to lie, cheat, or steal? By being an example before them of proper behavior. Jesus showed us by example what it means to lead a perfect life, despite the evil surrounding Him. "For we do not have a high priest who cannot sympathize with our weaknesses, but One who has been tempted in all things as we are, yet without sin" (Hebrews 4:15).

When Satan bombarded Christ during an intense time of temptation in the wilderness, Christ showed us how to repel such attacks successfully—through liberal use of the Word of God, prayer, and obedience.

*Lord, strengthen my faith today. Help me to
overcome the evil one's daily temptations.*

Israel Breaks the Covenant

*"I said, 'I will never break My covenant with you,
and as for you, you shall make no covenant with the
inhabitants of this land; you shall tear down their
altars.' But you have not obeyed Me."*

JUDGES 2:1–2

No sooner had the Israelites taken possession of their land
than they forgot all the Lord's admonitions.

God's hand was now against them for choosing to
worship idols instead of honoring Him. But God never
stopped loving these people He'd chosen. "When the LORD
raised up judges for them, the LORD was with the judge
and delivered them from the hand of their enemies all the
days of the judge; for the LORD was moved to pity by their
groaning because of those who oppressed and afflicted
them" (Judges 2:18).

For a while the people followed the judges, but as soon
as one of these leaders died, the Israelites sought out their
idols again.

So God left five enemy nations as strongholds within the
region to test Israel's obedience to His commandments (3:3).

*Lord, fill me with Your strength that I might not
backslide into the pit of disobedience again.*

A Discerning Woman

*Wisdom reposes in the heart of the discerning and even
among fools she lets herself be known.*

PROVERBS 14:33 NIV

Dorothy, a precious older woman, faithfully attended my
Bible study group each week despite the fact that she
suffered from congestive heart failure. She was the kind of
person one treasured as a gift, knowing the time with her
would be all too brief. She shared the contents of her heart
freely, no longer restricted behind the confining walls of
decorum. From her perspective, the word *cherish* didn't
exist in her husband's vocabulary.

We would pray and cry together over the grief her
marriage had caused her soul. And then she'd sit and
play a beautiful hymn on the piano. This was the way
the Lord ministered to her pain. Confident of her eternal
destination, she exuded serenity, wisdom, peace, and love.
Today's proverb says that "wisdom reposes in the heart of
the discerning." How well Dorothy understood this.

*Lord, everyone has a cross to bear. But because You bore
Calvary's cross for me, I have the hope of eternal life.*

When Will Christ Rapture the Faithful?

Now we request you, brethren, with regard to the coming of our Lord Jesus Christ and our gathering together to Him, that you not be quickly shaken from your composure or be disturbed either by a spirit or a message or a letter as if from us, to the effect that the day of the Lord has come. Let no one in any way deceive you.

2 THESSALONIANS 2:1–3

Paul and Timothy had founded the church at Thessalonica. For a time these Thessalonians remained strong. But then came persecution so severe that they were shaken to their roots. If these trial-filled days comprised their last moments on earth, where was the hope of being "caught up in Christ"? Paul wanted to dispel their misconceptions and correct several weaknesses in this church.

Before the antichrist bursts onto the world scene, there will be a great falling away from the truth (1 Timothy 4:1–3).

Even so, come, Lord Jesus!

Motives of the Heart

The LORD has made everything for its own purpose,
even the wicked for the day of evil.

PROVERBS 16:4

Horoscopes in newspapers and psychic telephone hotlines exist because people have a natural curiosity to know the future. Despite the phenomenal success of recent Hollywood blockbusters, I can assure you an attack by aliens is not on the horizon. No, our real threat will come from within the very real but unseen spiritual realm, not the extraterrestrial.

Surrounding us are beings from another world, but they belong to Satan. And their sole purpose is to seduce us into wavering from the truth. They dangle us from the scaffolding of unbelief. *Did God mean what He said? Doesn't He want us to have any fun? Do we really need Him telling us what to do?* Absolutely! Only God can give us a secure, peaceful, and perfect future—an eternal future in heaven with Him.

Lord, there have been times when I compromised the truth of Your Word. Please help me get back on track. Place my feet firmly on the pavement of Your Word.

Those Born of God Obey Him

*Whoever believes that Jesus is the Christ is born of God,
and whoever loves the Father loves the child born of Him.
By this we know that we love the children of God,
when we love God and observe His commandments.*

1 JOHN 5:1-2

When our children disobey, we feel not only extreme disappointment but a sense that they don't love us. For if they did, they would understand that our instructions are meant to guide them over the rough terrain of life. This is exactly how God feels when we fail to follow Him, for He equates love with obedience.

*Lord, when I'm wandering without purpose,
please bring me close to You.*

Finding the Messiah

He found first his own brother Simon and said to him,
"We have found the Messiah" (which translated means Christ).

JOHN 1:41

I'll never forget the day that I accepted Jesus Christ as my Savior. I'd been drawn to church twice that day, aware that my soul ached for peace. So many Christians had told me that all I needed to do was "pray and ask Christ into my life." But that seemed overly simplistic. How could this action change my life?

A short time before, while recovering from a compression fracture in my back, I began attending a Bible study. Now those scriptures I'd heard there began to come back to me. It wasn't a matter of reciting words. Instead, asking Christ into my life meant being willing to trade all the emptiness and estrangement within my soul for the completeness that He alone could provide.

Lord, I pray for strength to share Your love with unbelieving family members.

The Stone the Builders Rejected

*The stone which the builders rejected
has become the chief corner stone.*

PSALM 118:22

When a building is started, a cornerstone must be placed precisely because the rest of the structure is lined up with it. Likewise, Jesus Christ is the cornerstone of the Church. And His Church is comprised of both Jews and Gentiles, united as the Body of Christ and dependent upon Him for guidance.

Before the world began, God envisioned His Church. Jesus Christ, the Son, would come and die for its members so that they would be cleansed from sin. And Christ would be the very foundation upon which this Church would stand.

Is Jesus Christ the true cornerstone of your church? If you're looking for a church home, make sure you check the "foundation" first.

Lord Jesus Christ, You alone are to be the cornerstone of my life. Please help me to discard those concerns that block my view of You.

God's Protection for Widows

The LORD will tear down the house of the proud,
but He will establish the boundary of the widow.

PROVERBS 15:25

Christmas shopping preoccupied my father's thoughts as he picked out one special gift for each child, something he or she had wanted all year. But just after the last gift had been purchased, a severe heart attack overtook my dad.

My mother's first concern was how she might continue caring for her children, all ten of whom lived at home. No matter what her hardships, Mom has honored God, in whom she placed her faith and the care of her life. She's now been widowed far longer than the years she was married. She's raised her children, paid off her mortgage, and passed down her love of art to all her grandchildren.

Father, let me share Your Word with those women who now find themselves alone – "Now she who is a widow indeed and who has been left alone, has fixed her hope on God and continues in entreaties and prayers night and day" (1 Timothy 5:5).

An Angel Visits Ophrah

*Then the angel of the Lord came and sat under the oak
that was in Ophrah. . . . Gideon was beating out wheat in
the wine press in order to save it from the Midianites.
The angel of the Lord appeared to him and said to
him, "The Lord is with you, O valiant warrior."*

JUDGES 6:11–12

The Lord was about to sell a very surprised man named
Gideon on the idea of becoming Israel's next judge. God
knew Gideon longed for deliverance for Israel. Once again
the people of Israel had turned to their age-old sin of
idolatry.

Have you ever felt like the weight of the world rested
on your shoulders? Well, that's Gideon for you. "O Lord,
how shall I deliver Israel? Behold, my family is the least
in Manasseh, and I am the youngest in my father's house"
(Judges 6:15). The Lord answered Gideon with the same
resounding message of assurance that He always gives to
His servants: "Surely I will be with you" (6:16). God is with
us in the fight and that's enough!

Father, hold my hand today and every day.

God's Message to the Churches

*"But I have this against you,
that you have left your first love."*

REVELATION 2:4

One of my favorite questions to ask couples over dinner is "How did you meet?" Each story invariably presents a set of impossible circumstances that had to be orchestrated in order to bring this man and woman together. As these details are relayed, a glow begins to come back into the eyes of those remembering. There is nothing to compare with that "first bloom of love."

This is the kind of love that God desires from us. That on-fire, totally consuming, single focus of our attention. His call to the church at Ephesus then was that they remember their first love—and rekindle their purpose to seek Him first.

O Lord, may Your Light be the fire in my soul!

Knowing God's Precepts

Teach me Your statutes. Make me understand the way of Your precepts, so I will meditate on Your wonders. My soul weeps because of grief; strengthen me according to Your word. Remove the false way from me, and graciously grant me Your law.

PSALM 119:26–29

Martin Luther, an Augustinian monk, recognized that the precepts he learned from studying the scriptures didn't mesh with the teachings of the Roman Catholic Church. Therefore, in 1517, he openly stated his objections to the Catholic Church by nailing his Ninety-Five "Theses" to the door of the church at Wittenberg. This began the revival that led to the formation of the Protestant Church.

Confession of sin is the beginning of true hope. For when we acknowledge that we've failed, God can use our broken and contrite heart, through the Holy Spirit, to mold us anew.

Understand and walk in the way of His precepts by meditating on God's Word. If you're not participating in an in-depth Bible study, consider finding or starting one.

Lord, teach me Your ways, that I might live out Your precepts before my family and loved ones.

A Great Teacher

"Truly, truly, I say to you, unless one is born again he cannot see the kingdom of God."

JOHN 3:3

Nicodemus came to Christ under cover of darkness, at night. Although the Pharisees, the group of religious leaders to which he belonged, had reached the conclusion that Christ was sent from God, they hadn't bridged the gap to full understanding.

Nicodemus obviously heard what Christ had said and couldn't shake it loose from his thoughts. He sought the truth, so Christ made it as clear as a starlit night.

Later in the scriptures we see Nicodemus as the one who boldly risks his life to help Joseph of Arimathea take Christ's body from the cross. And Nicodemus brought an expensive "mixture of myrrh and aloes, about a hundred pounds weight. So they took the body of Jesus and bound it in linen wrappings with the spices, as is the burial custom of the Jews" (John 19:39–40).

Lord, You told Nicodemus he must be born again. I praise You that You are the God of second chances, the God of truth!

Strength Is Not in Numbers

The LORD said to Gideon, "The people who are with you
are too many for Me to give Midian into their hands,
for Israel would become boastful, saying, 'My own power
has delivered me.' Now therefore come, proclaim in the
hearing of the people, saying, 'Whoever is afraid and
trembling, let him return and depart from Mount Gilead.'"

JUDGES 7:2–3

Why can't we get it through our heads that if God is on our side, we don't need anyone else? Perhaps because we can't see Him.

Gideon had the same challenge. His own battle strategy included amassing a multitude that would obliterate the Midianites. And God told him no. God did not desire to perform a miracle that might be misconstrued as an act accomplished by human hands.

Instead, God had Gideon keep whittling down that number of troops. Finally, with a mere three hundred men, Gideon crossed the Jordan and won the battle. But the people who followed him still didn't understand.

Lord, have I watched Your hand of deliverance in my
own life only to become complacent? Help me repent!

Fearfully and Wonderfully Made

*For You formed my inward parts; You wove me in my
mother's womb. I will give thanks to You, for I am fearfully
and wonderfully made; wonderful are Your works,
and my soul knows it very well. My frame was not hidden
from You, when I was made in secret, and skillfully wrought
in the depths of the earth; Your eyes have seen my unformed
substance; and in Your book were all written the days
that were ordained for me, when as yet
there was not one of them.*

PSALM 139:13–16

Each of us has not only an inborn sense that there is a God
but also an understanding that we possess a designed
intent. Your parents aren't responsible for your creation;
God is. Had He not willed your very existence, you would
not have happened. God wants to use your life to further
His kingdom.

*Lord, please renew my understanding that You
created me in Your own image and likeness
with a body, mind, and spirit.*

Absolute Assurance of Eternal Life

"He who believes in the Son has eternal life;
but he who does not obey the Son will not see life,
but the wrath of God abides on him."

JOHN 3:36

Rigo Lopez sought assurance alone in a motel room as he surveyed the shattered pieces of his life. He'd just left his second wife and his children. Tears rolled down his cheeks and he had no answers.

He turned on the TV, and by the grace of God, Billy Graham's voice carried a message of hope. "You can have absolute assurance today of your salvation," Graham preached. Those words went directly to the source of pain in Rigo's heart. Rigo then prayed, "God, give me that assurance. Help me to know that You can forgive me and salvage the ruins of my life."

Rigo returned to his family and began again. He studied and eventually taught the Bible to others. The Word of God says that we can have absolute assurance of eternal life today. Rigo grasped onto God's truth and his life was transformed.

Lord, I am assured of my salvation. Help me share this absolute truth with those in despair.

Spirit of God or Spirit of Antichrist?

The eyes of the LORD are toward the righteous
and His ears are open to their cry.

PSALM 34:15

This morning I read the following scripture: "FOR THE EYES OF THE LORD ARE TOWARD THE RIGHTEOUS, AND HIS EARS ATTEND TO THEIR PRAYER, BUT THE FACE OF THE LORD IS AGAINST THOSE WHO DO EVIL" (1 Peter 3:12). The Spirit of God heard my cry and took my petition before the Father who answers my prayer, for I have confessed belief in Him.

Anyone who has discarded the commands of God, is not God's child. "You are from God, little children, and have overcome them; because greater is He who is in you than he who is in the world. They are from the world; therefore they speak as from the world, and the world listens to them" (1 John 4:4–5).

Lord, guide me in this last hour so that I will continue to spread the Gospel and not walk away.

Encounter at the Well

There came a woman of Samaria to draw water.
Jesus said to her, "Give Me a drink."
JOHN 4:7

Here lived a woman of ill repute. She was shunned by those who led wholesome lives. After all, she had had five husbands and now lived with a man, unmarried.

Although Jewish men didn't speak to women in public, Jesus asked this woman for a drink of water. Shocked, the woman responded, "How is it that You, being a Jew, ask me for a drink since I am a Samaritan woman?" (John 4:9).

Jesus Christ goes right to the heart of her problem. "If you knew the gift of God, and who it is who says to you, 'Give Me a drink,' you would have asked Him, and He would have given you living water" (4:10). And when she asked where to get this living water, He explained the gift of eternal life to her.

Father, help me to seek out those who for whatever reason
are shunned and despised. They need You so much.

He Is Coming with the Clouds

BEHOLD, HE IS COMING WITH THE CLOUDS, and every eye will see Him, even those who pierced Him; and all the tribes of the earth will mourn over Him. So it is to be. Amen.

REVELATION 1:7

Cecil B. DeMille was known for his extravagant movie productions. Who can forget his version of Moses parting the Red Sea? However, the appearance of Christ in the clouds will surpass every event that has ever taken place on earth. This future event will be a worldwide phenomenon in which every eye will see Him. And the hearts of those who refused to examine the evidence and refused to know Him will ache with the agonizing pain of conviction that it's simply too late. The purpose for His appearance this time will be to judge the world for its greatest sin, the rejection of His great gift of salvation.

Father, when humans have failed me I tend to blame You for their choices. Please break down the barriers in my heart that I might worship You.

All Is Vanity!

The words of the Preacher, the son of David, king in
Jerusalem. "Vanity of vanities," says the Preacher,
"vanity of vanities! All is vanity."

ECCLESIASTES 1:1-2

At the end of his life, King Solomon, who is thought to be the writer of Ecclesiastes, concludes that the things of earth are but fleeting. Perhaps you, too, are prone to reflect on the tasks that occupy your days, concluding that nothing gets accomplished.

As we go through Ecclesiastes, Solomon repeatedly uses two key word pictures, "meaningless" and "under the sun." As king over Israel he had seen "all the works which have been done under the sun, and behold, all is vanity and striving after wind. . . . Because in much wisdom there is much grief, and increasing knowledge results in increasing pain" (Ecclesiastes 1:14, 18). Solomon had experienced the best the world has to offer. . .and it wasn't enough.

Lord, as I begin to learn the truths contained in this book,
please help me view my priorities from Your perspective.

Healed Miraculously

*Now there is in Jerusalem by the sheep gate a pool. . .
having five porticoes. In these lay a multitude of those who
were sick, blind, lame, and withered, [waiting for the moving
of the waters; for an angel of the Lord went down at certain
seasons into the pool and stirred up the water; whoever then
first, after the stirring up of the water, stepped in was made
well from whatever disease with which he was afflicted.]*
JOHN 5:2–4

So many times when we cry out to the Lord for healing, He
seems to be asking us the same question He posed to the
man who had been sitting at this gate for thirty-eight years
waiting for healing: "Do you wish to get well?" (John 5:6).

In other words, do you honestly desire to rid yourself
of the things that debilitate you? For true healing of our
souls requires a change of direction.

*Lord, if sin is at the root of my infirmity, then bring me to
swift repentance. But if my suffering is to point others
toward Your glory, quench my thirst with Your living water.*

Unremarkable Lives

Then Jephthah the Gileadite died and was buried in one of the cities of Gilead. Now Ibzan of Bethlehem judged Israel after him.

JUDGES 12:7–8

What do you want etched into your own tombstone? Personally, I'd like to be remembered this way: "Studied the Word of God diligently and cared about bringing it to others."

But no such accolades are recorded for the four judges Jephthah, Ibzan, Elon, and Abdon. Jephthah is known mainly for his "rash vow," while Ibzan's claim to fame is a large family, whom he married off to the pagans dwelling in that area. Nothing is learned about Abdon except that "he had forty sons and thirty grandsons who rode on seventy donkeys" (Judges 12:14).

How can we discern the will of God for our lives? Daily prayer is definitely the main source. And this involves not only relating our needs to God, but also listening for His directions. For He never meant for us to traverse through this maze called life without the road maps He would supply.

Lord, remind me to linger in prayer, listening for Your voice.

Jesus, Bread of Life

"As the living Father sent Me, and I live because of the
Father, so he who eats Me, he also will live because of Me.
This is the bread which came down out of heaven;
not as the fathers ate and died; he who eats
this bread will live forever."

JOHN 6:57-58

Some said that Jesus' teachings were too difficult to even
bother with, while others stated that Christ was speaking
about cannibalism. But the majority just walked away,
refusing to follow Christ anymore. To continue following
Him required faith and commitment.

To truly partake of Christ is to accept Him as He is,
fully God and fully man, sent from God, recognizing our
need for Him. He came first to the Jews, but they refused
the message. What is your response?

Lord, when I don't understand the scriptures,
Your Holy Spirit will provide me with comprehension.

The Father Has Bestowed a Great Love

*When He appears, we will be like Him, because we will see
Him just as He is. And everyone who has this hope fixed
on Him purifies himself, just as He is pure.*

1 JOHN 3:2–3

While we don't know when Jesus is coming again,
we do know that the receiving of our new bodies will
coincide with this event. "When Christ, who is our life, is
revealed, then you also will be revealed with Him in glory"
(Colossians 3:4).

Yet the gift of our new bodies is only one aspect of the
Father's incredible love for His children. His love prompts
His children to purify themselves just as He is pure (1 John
3:3). They also abide in Him and practice righteousness
(3:6–7), for they have been born of God (3:9; John 3:7).

*Lord, the greatest gift I can lay before You is an act of my
will that makes me Your child. Yes, I have been born again.*

Not Even His Brothers Believed

Therefore His brothers said to Him, "Leave here and go into Judea, so that Your disciples also may see Your works which You are doing. For no one does anything in secret when he himself seeks to be known publicly. If You do these things, show Yourself to the world." For not even His brothers were believing in Him.

JOHN 7:3–5

One of the most difficult challenges any believer faces is reaching family with Christ's message. Although Jesus' own brothers had daily viewed His sinless life, they were as blind as the Pharisees to who He really was. Surely these siblings, Christ's earthly half brothers (Matthew 13:55–56; Mark 6:1–6), knew that the Jews were seeking to kill Him (John 7:1). But they were headed for Jerusalem to attend the Feast of Booths, as required by God. Jesus' brothers were embarking on a journey to a religious feast and yet rejecting their own Messiah.

Christ's half brothers were completely in tune with the world and not with God.

Thank You, Jesus, for reminding me to wait for God's timing in my life, especially when the pressure applied by others would have me rush on ahead.

A Time to Mourn

*There is an appointed time for everything. And there is
a time for every event under heaven. . .a time to weep
and a time to laugh; a time to mourn and a time to dance.*

ECCLESIASTES 3:1, 4

Somehow we reach the faulty conclusion that if God loves us, all negative incidents are nixed. Do we doubt that the Father loved the Son and yet allowed the Son to suffer a cruel death on the cross? The penalty for sin was death, a penalty that had to be paid by someone absolutely sinless in order for us to be forgiven. Only Jesus Christ could fill that role.

If Christ Himself suffered, then why should we be immune from all maladies?

Occasionally a time of mourning enters our lives, sometimes stealing in almost silently, sometimes brashly breaking down the door to our well-constructed sense of security. Neither path reflects nor distorts the fact that God loves us. But tragedy and mourning are both part of the ebb and flow of the "rhythm of life."

*Lord, through my veil of tears help me to view Your rescuing
hand, that I might reach out to grasp You more firmly.*

Christ Eliminated All Ethnic Barriers

There is no distinction between Greek and Jew,
circumcised and uncircumcised, barbarian, Scythian,
slave and freeman, but Christ is all, and in all.

COLOSSIANS 3:11

To say we love Christ and yet maintain deeply rooted prejudices against others is inconsistent with everything He taught. For Christ came to reconcile all peoples to Himself, not separate us into factions.

Above all, God wants us to be harmonious in worship of Him and also in working with Him. "Now may the God who gives perseverance and encouragement grant you to be of the same mind with one another according to Christ Jesus, so that with one accord you may with one voice glorify the God and Father of our Lord Jesus Christ. Therefore, accept one another, just as Christ also accepted us to the glory of God" (Romans 15:5–7).

Lord, let true peace, which is Christ, be found in my heart
as I am obedient to Your command to love one another,
just as You have loved me (John 13:34).

The Days of Your Youth

Remember also your Creator in the days of your youth,
before the evil days come and the years draw near when
you will say, "I have no delight in them."... Fear God and
keep His commandments, because this applies to every
person. For God will bring every act to judgment,
everything which is hidden, whether it is good or evil.

ECCLESIASTES 12:1, 13–14

Most of us have encountered women who freely share biblical truths "handed down to them" from their grandmothers or mothers. Is the faith being displayed in their lives?

The book of Ecclesiastes concludes with the admonition not only to remember our Creator when we are young, but to continue following His precepts throughout our time on earth.

Have you forgotten the God of your youth? Have His principles been compromised away by the pressures of a world that teaches that the Ten Commandments are optional? With the Lord's help, it's not too late to turn it all around.

Lord, if I look back and see a trail of regret,
please give me the courage to change the view.

Hold to God's Truth

*For you have died and your life is hidden with Christ
in God. When Christ, who is our life, is revealed,
then you also will be revealed with Him in glory.
Therefore consider the members of your earthly body
as dead to immorality, impurity, passion, evil desire,
and greed, which amounts to idolatry.*

COLOSSIANS 3:3–5

Some Christian testimonies really stir your heart. Some are
from individuals who have turned from lives of debauchery
and waste to become true seekers of God. Our churches
are comprised of redeemed sinners.

Paul's message is that Christ in us should cause a
change in our lives, for we have been delivered from the
"wrath of God." This metamorphosis should make a visible
difference in how we are living our lives, for Christ has set
up residence within us.

*Let me be cautious of bypassing the Word of God and the
Spirit of God to substitute visions of angels for the Gospel.*

Ruth, Faithful Daughter-in-Law

Then Elimelech, Naomi's husband, died; and she was left with her two sons. They took for themselves Moabite women as wives; the name of the one was Orpah and the name of the other Ruth. And they lived there about ten years.

RUTH 1:3–4

Ruth was a young woman when her husband died. In one of the greatest testaments of love in the Bible, she chose to remain with her widowed mother-in-law, Naomi, even choosing to believe in her God.

Few daughters-in-law would have persisted in devotion to a woman whose life held such abysmal tragedy and so little prospect for positive change. However, God had a glorious plan. "Now Naomi had a kinsman of her husband, a man of great wealth, of the family of Elimelech, whose name was Boaz" (Ruth 2:1).

Ruth gathered leftover grain from Boaz's fields so that she and Naomi might have food. And Boaz showed her favor. In time, Ruth would become Boaz's bride and mother to his son, a son whose lineage would include David and the Messiah, Jesus Christ.

Lord, may I learn from Ruth's example of abiding love.

God Stands by His Word

"Behold, I am going to send My messenger, and he will clear the way before Me. And the Lord, whom you seek, will suddenly come to His temple; and the messenger of the covenant, in whom you delight, behold, He is coming," says the LORD of hosts.

MALACHI 3:1

God always keeps His promises. Through Moses, God had warned the nation of Israel that if they refused to obey, they would be taken into captivity. In 586 BC, this prophecy was fulfilled.

God spoke through the prophet Jeremiah, giving the exact duration of this captivity as seventy years. This is the number of years Israel remained in Babylon.

Today's scripture reveals two specific messages. First, a messenger will precede the Messiah, announcing Him to Israel. This would be John the Baptist (Luke 1:76).

Next, the Messiah will "come to His temple."

Jesus Christ, God's promise to the world, has come! Thank You for Your Word of Truth.

Where Is the Promise of His Coming?

*Know this first of all, that in the last days mockers will
come with their mocking, following after their own lusts,
and saying, "Where is the promise of His coming?
For ever since the fathers fell asleep, all continues just
as it was from the beginning of creation." For when they
maintain this, it escapes their notice that by the word of
God the heavens existed long ago and the earth was
formed out of water and by water, through which the world
at that time was destroyed, being flooded with water.*

2 PETER 3:3–6

How can a loving God destroy the very men and women
and their world that He created? Look at how much time
He provided for them to repent. From the time Noah
received the order from God to build the ark until the rain
began, a span of 120 years had elapsed. Certainly this was
time enough for everyone to hear the prediction and take
appropriate action.

*Today I will repent of my sins. And if I'm not
entirely sure I've done so, today I will claim
Jesus to be my Savior and Lord.*

Jesus, the Good Shepherd

"But he who enters by the door is a shepherd of the sheep.
To him the doorkeeper opens, and the sheep hear his voice,
and he calls his own sheep by name and leads them out."

JOHN 10:2-3

In our day we hear some who defend their heinous acts by saying, "Voices told me to do it." Certainly the one they chose to listen to was not the voice of Jesus Christ, for He cannot contradict Himself. True sheep listen only for the voice of their Shepherd.

God calls us by name, just as the shepherd has pet names for his sheep. Someday, when the King of kings, our Good Shepherd, calls us home to heaven, we'll hear the name He calls us.

Lord, guide me to safe pastures today.
Never leave me.

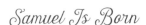

Samuel Is Born

It came about in due time, after Hannah had conceived,
that she gave birth to a son; and she named him Samuel,
*saying, "Because I have asked him of the L*ORD*."*

1 SAMUEL 1:20

Hannah, a woman of real faith, wanted to keep her promise
to God. After Samuel was born and she had weaned him,
she took him promptly to the temple.

Every year Hannah and Elkanah returned for their
sacrifice at the temple, and every year Hannah brought
Samuel a new robe to wear. For her faithfulness, God
blessed Hannah with three more sons and two daughters
(1 Samuel 2:21).

God was now training Samuel to take over as judge
of Israel, as Eli's own sons had no regard for the Lord. As
Samuel continued to grow "in favor both with the LORD
and with men" (2:26), the Lord declared, "Those who
honor me I will honor, but those who despise me will be
disdained" (2:30 NIV).

Lord, if You should give me a child, guide me as
You guided Hannah—to sincere faithfulness.

Isaiah, a Major Prophet

The vision of Isaiah the son of Amoz concerning Judah and Jerusalem, which he saw during the reigns of Uzziah, Jotham, Ahaz and Hezekiah, kings of Judah. Listen, O heavens, and hear, O earth; for the LORD speaks, "Sons I have reared and brought up, but they have revolted against Me.... My people do not understand."

ISAIAH 1:1–3

Reading Isaiah provides a necessary heart check. Like Israel, if we fail to turn from our defiant ways, we must ask, "Where will you be stricken again, as you continue in your rebellion? The whole head is sick and the whole heart is faint. From the sole of the foot even to the head there is nothing sound in it, only bruises, welts and raw wounds, not pressed out or bandaged, nor softened with oil" (Isaiah 1:5–6).

Lord, the book of Isaiah displays Your promises and prophecies. Open my mind to receive Your truth. And keep me from confusion, that I might know You as both Messiah and Lord.

Jesus Raises Lazarus

Now a certain man was sick, Lazarus of
Bethany. . . . So the sisters sent word to Him,
saying, "Lord, behold, he whom You love is sick."
JOHN 11:1, 3

Lazarus was about to breathe his last. And yet Christ seemed to be denying the gravity of the situation. Jesus took His time getting there, four days as a matter of fact. And when He did arrive, Lazarus had been buried! Now Christ was only a few miles away from Bethany. It took all the human restraint He possessed not to run to Lazarus's aid. But Jesus has, as always, a greater purpose.

At the tomb of His friend, Jesus called, "Lazarus, come forth" (John 11:43). And Lazarus arose from the tomb and walked out, his grave clothes dangling from his body. Have you allowed Christ to exercise His authority to bring you forth to new life?

Lord, strengthen my faith so that when tragedy strikes,
I know that You are the Resurrection and the Life.

Hannah Acknowledges Her Savior

*Then Hannah prayed and said, "My heart exults in
the L*ORD*; my horn is exalted in the L*ORD*, my mouth speaks
boldly against my enemies, because I rejoice in
Your salvation. There is no one holy like the
L*ORD*, indeed, there is no one besides You."*

1 SAMUEL 2:1–2

Hannah spent her time in the temple, praying and serving
others. And God granted the deepest longing of her heart,
despite the fact that she was just a sinner who could offer
God nothing but her brokenness and yielded spirit.

Hannah refers to her Savior as a "God of knowledge,"
for she revered or honored His Word (1 Samuel 2:3). She
took to heart all that God had done for her people in
the past and accepted that He alone could change her
circumstances. To whom do you turn for solutions?

*Lord, You alone can lift me from the depths of despair
and set me on high places.*

Stand Firm and Receive the Crown

Therefore, my beloved brethren whom I long to see,
my joy and crown, in this way stand firm in the Lord,
my beloved. I urge Euodia and I urge Syntyche
to live in harmony in the Lord.
PHILIPPIANS 4:1–2

Evidently, two of the women at the church in Philippi, Euodia and Syntyche, were living less than harmoniously. Therefore, Paul admonished them.

It is significant that Paul took the time to address this issue. Left unchecked, such arguing would wreak havoc in the church. Perhaps you have encountered someone who, although she professes belief in Christ, has treated you without charity or love. Fast, pray for guidance, and then go to her and pray again. Failure to do so gives Satan an opportunity to get a foothold within the church as the argument escalates and people choose sides.

Lord, help me to remember that You surrendered all Your
rights that I might know true freedom. Please show me
how to persevere, make amends, and live in harmony.

His Light Dispels Darkness

And Jesus cried out and said, "He who believes in Me,
does not believe in Me but in Him who sent Me.
He who sees Me sees the One who sent Me. I have
come as Light into the world, so that everyone who
believes in Me will not remain in darkness."

JOHN 12:44-46

How people can read the Word of God and reach such
faulty conclusions mystifies me. If you have a question
about one verse of scripture, first, you need to pray that
God's Spirit will provide enlightenment. Then get a good
study Bible that has cross-referencing on each page along
with the text.

Next, invest in or borrow a theological text from your
church library that deals with the Bible book you are
studying. Ask your pastors or ministers for their personal
recommendations. With such guidance, God's Word
becomes clearer and your faith is sure to deepen.

Your truth is readily available, Lord. Therefore,
I know with certainty that I will one day see You
face-to-face. Deepen my faith so that I might
penetrate the spiritual darkness around me.

Being of One Mind

---

*Do nothing from selfishness or empty conceit,
but with humility of mind regard one another as more
important than yourselves; do not merely look out for your
own personal interests, but also for the interests of others.*

PHILIPPIANS 2:3-4

As Christians, we are called to encourage one another in the faith. Paul, who spent so much of his own life in prison, had a deep understanding of the need for the reassurance and hope that the Lord richly supplies. This reliance on God's abundant source of blessings overflowed from his heart, spilling out to his fellow Christians.

What if in church we used the greeting time during the worship service to find out the specific needs within the Body of Christ? Many of our brothers and sisters are wounded, both physically and spiritually. Yet they come to Sunday services with a deceptive smile on their faces, their return trip home as lonely as the rest of their week will probably be. Do you care?

*Who is my source of strength?
Lord, help me encourage others.*

The Meaning of True Christian Fellowship

I thank my God in all my remembrance of you,
always offering prayer with joy in my every prayer
for you all, in view of your participation in the
gospel from the first day until now.

PHILIPPIANS 1:3–5

Paul's joy is not dependent upon circumstances. Rather, it overflows from the content of his heart, where the true source of joy resides, Jesus Christ. And because of this indwelling, Paul senses a oneness with other believers despite the fact that they are far from him. It is the love of Christ that binds them together.

Paul's only aim in life was to be where God wanted him—so that he might spread the Gospel to all who would listen. And if this aspiration required suffering and isolation on his part, then Paul gladly paid the price.

Lord, might I pray as Paul, "I press on toward
the goal for the prize of the upward call of God
in Christ Jesus" (Philippians 3:14).

Jesus' Last Passover

Jesus, knowing that the Father had given all things into His hands, and that He had come forth from God and was going back to God, got up from supper, and laid aside His garments; and taking a towel, He girded Himself. Then He poured water into the basin, and began to wash the disciples' feet.

JOHN 13:3–5

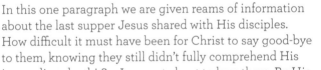

In this one paragraph we are given reams of information about the last supper Jesus shared with His disciples. How difficult it must have been for Christ to say good-bye to them, knowing they still didn't fully comprehend His impending death! So Jesus set about to love them. By His example, He wanted to show them that they were called likewise to be servants.

Christ began washing the dust from the disciples' feet. Usually a servant would administer this kindness to those who came in for the banquet supper. But the God who had created them desired that His followers know the depth of His humility.

Lord, help me to cultivate the heart of a true servant.

Jesus, the True Vine

"I am the true vine, and My Father is the vinedresser.
Every branch in Me that does not bear fruit, He takes away;
and every branch that bears fruit, He prunes it so that it
may bear more fruit. You are already clean because of the
word which I have spoken to you. Abide in Me, and I in you.
As the branch cannot bear fruit of itself unless it abides
in the vine, so neither can you unless you abide in Me.
I am the vine, you are the branches; he who
abides in Me and I in him, he bears much fruit,
for apart from Me you can do nothing."

JOHN 15:1–5

Christ used word pictures to clarify concepts for His followers. And this parable about the vine and the branches was extremely familiar to them.

This same offer to abide in the vine is extended to all who hear the Gospel message. Have you responded? And how diligently are you abiding?

Lord, help me to abide in You.

A New Name for Israel

For Zion's sake I will not keep silent, and for Jerusalem's sake I will not keep quiet, until her righteousness goes forth like brightness, and her salvation like a torch that is burning. The nations will see your righteousness, and all kings your glory; and you will be called by a new name which the mouth of the LORD will designate.

ISAIAH 62:1–2

Whenever God sets about to perform a work of regeneration, He also provides a new name. For instance, Abraham was known simply as Abram prior to God's promise that he would be the father of a "multitude of nations" (Genesis 17:5).

Similarly, God changed Jacob's name to Israel, and he became the father of the twelve tribes of Israel (Genesis 32:28).

*Lord, my name remains the same,
but my heart is forever changed by Your love.*

Peter, an Apostle of Jesus Christ

Peter, an apostle of Jesus Christ, to those who reside as aliens. . .who are chosen according to the foreknowledge of God the Father, by the sanctifying work of the Spirit, to obey Jesus Christ and be sprinkled with His blood: May grace and peace be yours in the fullest measure.
1 PETER 1:1–2

The only true "superhero" is Jesus Christ, who will never fail us. He alone was fully God and fully man. Therefore, He alone possesses perfectly all the characteristics we most admire. For He remains faithful, just, loving, omnipotent, and eternal.

Peter doesn't seek position or power. Instead, he humbly admonishes his hearers to "obey Christ," on whom Peter also depends.

The name Peter, or Petra, means "rock."
Help my faith, Lord, to be rock solid and unwavering.

A Husband's Love

*Wives, be subject to your own husbands, as to the Lord.
For the husband is the head of the wife, as Christ also
is the head of the church, He Himself being the Savior
of the body. But as the church is subject to Christ, so also
the wives ought to be to their husbands in everything.*

EPHESIANS 5:22-24

It's critical to remember that God intended marriage to be
a partnership. We need to build one another up.

"So husbands ought also to love their own wives as
their own bodies" (Ephesians 5:28). If men truly loved their
wives to this degree, there probably isn't a woman alive
who'd run from it.

So what can we do to make things better? Pray. . .every
single day. But especially when things are out of kilter.
Know that God is vitally interested in the success of your
marriage, and act accordingly.

*Lord, I know that only You are capable of loving perfectly.
So the next time my marriage feels like a 90/10 proposition,
please remind me that You're giving 100 percent.*

Jeremiah's Revival

Now the word of the LORD came to me saying,
"Before I formed you in the womb I knew you,
and before you were born I consecrated you;
I have appointed you a prophet to the nations."

JEREMIAH 1:4-5

Jeremiah prophesied prior to and during Babylon's three sieges of Judah. Revival came when the Word of the Lord was found in the house of God and Josiah, the last king of Judah, called the people to repentance. However, following this great time of worship, Israel's disobedience once again set in, bringing upon the people yet again God's heavy hand of judgment. And Jeremiah the prophet wept.

Lord, I pray for answers to the dilemmas that plague
our society. Not knowing whom You have called for
special service, let me respect and revere each life
with hope, anticipation, and gratitude.

Sealed by the Holy Spirit

In Him, you also, after listening to the message of truth,
the gospel of your salvation—having also believed,
you were sealed in Him with the Holy Spirit of promise,
who is given as a pledge of our inheritance, with a view
to the redemption of God's own possession,
to the praise of His glory.

EPHESIANS 1:13–14

The apostle Paul penned the letter to the Ephesians between AD 60 and 62 while he was a prisoner in Rome. Ephesus, the fourth largest city in the Roman Empire, was steeped in idolatrous worship.

Into this spiritual darkness God sent Paul. The Lord desired to use this cultural setting to call out for Himself a church so that He could shine the light of truth upon this evil place.

Lord, there are dark places today that cry out for
Your redeeming light. Lead me to share Your
Word where it is needed desperately.

Question the Witnesses

The high priest then questioned Jesus about His disciples, and about His teaching. Jesus answered him, "I have spoken openly to the world; I always taught in synagogues and in the temple, where all the Jews come together; and I spoke nothing in secret. Why do you question Me? Question those who have heard what I spoke to them; they know what I said."

JOHN 18:19-21

Jesus Christ didn't come for a few souls; He presented the Gospel message openly for all to hear. Teaching in the Jewish temple, which was frequented not only by those who sought knowledge but also by those in search of an explanation of the truth, Jesus provided both.

As we go out into a world that is hostile to the Gospel message, there are those who listen to our testimony and then draw near to its refreshing waters. Others vow that nothing will force them to make a life change. And then there are those who deny the metamorphosis has even taken place. Their hearts are closed to receive the truth.

Lord, break down my walls of stubbornness that prevent me from hearing, seeing, and rallying to Your message.

What Constitutes Dynamic Faith?

*You see that faith was working with his works,
and as a result of the works, faith was perfected;
and the Scripture was fulfilled which says,
"AND ABRAHAM BELIEVED GOD, AND IT WAS RECKONED
TO HIM AS RIGHTEOUSNESS," and he was
called the friend of God.*
JAMES 2:22-23

Abraham's faith was evident by his actions. The very foundation of Abraham's faith was the Word of God. And no matter what God required of him, Abraham obeyed God. Therefore, all of his actions were born out of the call God had on his life.

"So faith comes from hearing, and hearing by the word of Christ" (Romans 10:17). This kind of dynamic faith involves the whole person. If someone professes their belief in God and yet does not take the Word to others, and refuses to attend a weekly Bible study, and can't be bothered to help those in obvious need, it makes me wonder whether that faith is real. For there has to be some outward manifestation of the change that takes place inwardly.

Lord, show me by Your Word how to reflect dynamic faith.

A Promise of Unity

"At that time they will call Jerusalem 'The Throne of the Lord,' and all the nations will be gathered to it."

JEREMIAH 3:17

In the year 586 BC, Solomon's temple was utterly destroyed. At the same time, the ark of the covenant was lost. God's glory had departed from Israel. For this reason, God's confirmation that Jerusalem would once again become the center for worship became critically important. During King Herod's reign the temple was rebuilt, fulfilling part of this prophecy. And when Jesus Christ came, it had once again become the center of worship.

True peace will reign in Israel when Christ returns again to earth (Matthew 24:29–39). Lord, help me wait!

Crown of Mockery

Pilate then took Jesus and scourged Him. And the soldiers
twisted together a crown of thorns and put it on His head,
and put a purple robe on Him; and they began to
come up to Him and say, "Hail, King of the Jews!"
and to give Him slaps in the face.

JOHN 19:1–3

The soldiers pretended to shower Jesus with all the
outward trappings of royalty. But this homage was one of
cruel mockery. The thorns were razor-sharp briars about
an inch and a half long. We can only imagine the taunting
voices of these men, triumphant glances spreading across
their faces as they pressed this crown into Christ's head
until blood ran down His face.

Lord, in my behalf You withstood extreme torture.
Am I adding new but invisible wounds each time
I refuse to crown You King of my own life?

Jonathan, Faithful to the End

Now the Philistines were fighting against Israel,
and the men of Israel fled from before the Philistines
and fell slain on Mount Gilboa. The Philistines overtook
Saul and his sons; and the Philistines killed Jonathan
and Abinadab and Malchi-shua the sons of Saul.

1 SAMUEL 31:1–2

Who has faithfully stood beside you through life's triumphs and tragedies? For David, this person was Jonathan.

Jonathan walked a tightrope, remaining faithful to God; to Saul, his father; and to David. Considering Saul's obsession with killing David, this task took on monstrous proportions.

Father, help me to be a faithful, loving,
and unforgettable friend.

James, Bond Servant of God

*James, a bond-servant of God and of the Lord Jesus
Christ, to the twelve tribes who are dispersed abroad:
Greetings. Consider it all joy, my brethren,
when you encounter various trials, knowing that
the testing of your faith produces endurance.*

JAMES 1:1–3

James had taken Christ for granted. Jesus' sinless life
had been lived out before him and yet James had not
responded to the invitation for salvation.

James finally understood his position in Christ, that
of a servant. He had successfully journeyed from a place
of hindering the Gospel, unaware of the time constraints
Christ had with the Father, to a place of understanding
the true source of wisdom (John 7:1–5). The apostle Paul
relates that James, along with Peter and John, became
one of the chief leaders of the church in Jerusalem
(Galatians 2:9).

*How grateful I am, Lord, that You're not willing that any
should perish, especially those of Your own family.*

David Learns of Saul's Death

"Saul and Jonathan his son are dead also."
2 SAMUEL 1:4

A young Amalekite man had related to David that Saul and Jonathan were dead. Then he confessed that Saul had been impaled on his own sword and begged him to kill him. After complying with this request, the Amalekite then removed the crown from Saul's head and the bracelet that was on his arm and brought these royal ornaments to David.

First, David led Israel in a time of mourning for Saul (2 Samuel 1:11–12). Following this expression of sorrow came a time of retribution (1:14–15).

David poured forth his personal anguish by writing a song for Saul and Jonathan. One verse reads, "Saul and Jonathan, beloved and pleasant in their life, and in their death they were not parted; they were swifter than eagles, they were stronger than lions" (1:23).

Lord, what an example David was, as he refused to gloat over Saul's death. David turned to You and requested guidance, and You gave him a fresh call to leadership. I rejoice!

Ezekiel's Call

*On the fifth of the month in the fifth year of King
Jehoiachin's exile, the word of the LORD came
expressly to Ezekiel the priest, son of Buzi.*

EZEKIEL 1:2-3

Sometimes God's plans are so different from what we
expect to be doing with our lives that it's really astonishing.

Although he was only eighteen years old when
some of the nobles and princes were captured by King
Nebuchadnezzar and taken from Judah to Babylon, Ezekiel
had already been groomed for the priesthood.

Ezekiel's life plan became forever altered ten years
later, in 597 BC, when he was among those taken in
Nebuchadnezzar's second siege against Jerusalem. Never
again would he view the temple where he had hoped to
serve God. However, when he was thirty years old, the Lord
gave him a vision of a new temple and another Jerusalem.
His call was to prophesy concerning Judah and Jerusalem,
Israel's coming restoration, and the temple.

Ezekiel's visions parallel those John recorded in
Revelation. These dreams show that no matter how bleak
Israel's present situation might be, their future would be
bright.

*Lord, as I read the prophecies of Ezekiel,
fill me with expectation!*

Always a Remnant

"'So as I live,' declares the Lord GOD, 'surely, because you have defiled My sanctuary with all your detestable idols and with all your abominations, therefore I will also withdraw, and My eye will have no pity and I will not spare.'"

EZEKIEL 5:11

Only the nation of Israel has managed to survive being scattered all over the globe and then come back to become a world power. How is this possible? God always preserves a remnant of His people. And it will be so until the end of time on this earth.

But how do we know this cycle will continue until the end of time? Four angels stand ready to execute God's judgment on the whole world. And they are restrained from action until "one hundred and forty-four thousand [are] sealed from every tribe of the sons of Israel" (Revelation 7:4). Twelve thousand from each of the tribes of Israel will be marked by God's own hand.

Many terrible plagues and judgments will take place upon the earth. However, God will bring this remnant of Israel safely through it all.

Father, I rejoice in Your Word: "And then He will send forth the angels, and will gather together His elect" (Mark 13:27).

A False Peace

"So My hand will be against the prophets who see false visions and utter lying divinations. They will have no place in the council of My people, nor will they be written down in the register of the house of Israel, nor will they enter the land of Israel, that you may know that I am the Lord GOD. It is definitely because they have misled My people by saying, 'Peace!' when there is no peace."

EZEKIEL 13:9-10

People today get sick of hearing modern doomsday forecasters who shout, "Turn or burn." Those living in Ezekiel's day reacted the same way. They preferred to listen to those who preached a message of peace rather than the need for repentance.

Just as Ezekiel could not remain complacent in the midst of false peace givers, those of our own day who know the truth are obligated to bring the message of repentance and salvation to others. How else will they hear and respond?

Lord, help me to share Your truth or assist others to do so, even in the midst of an apathetic and, yes, hostile world.

David's Rock, Fortress, and Deliverer

*"The LORD is my rock and my fortress and my deliverer;
my God, my rock, in whom I take refuge, my shield and
the horn of my salvation, my stronghold and my
refuge; my savior, You save me from violence."*

2 SAMUEL 22:2–3

David depended on the Lord as his Rock of faith. "Let the words of my mouth and the meditation of my heart be acceptable in Your sight, O LORD, my rock and my Redeemer" (Psalm 19:14).

However, to those who choose not to believe, Christ becomes only a stumbling block. "But Israel, pursuing a law of righteousness, did not arrive at that law. Why? Because they did not pursue it by faith, but as though it were by works. They stumbled over the stumbling stone, just as it is written, 'BEHOLD, I LAY IN ZION A STONE OF STUMBLING AND A ROCK OF OFFENSE, AND HE WHO BELIEVES IN HIM WILL NOT BE DISAPPOINTED' " (Romans 9:31–33).

*I praise You only, Jesus,
my Rock of Faith and Redeemer.*

Baptism of Repentance

"Repent, and each of you be baptized in the name of Jesus Christ for the forgiveness of your sins; and you will receive the gift of the Holy Spirit."

ACTS 2:38

Many of us were christened or baptized as infants. While this is a beautiful as well as meaningful service, such a rite does not cleanse a person from sin.

Jesus said, "The time is fulfilled, and the kingdom of God is at hand; repent and believe in the gospel" (Mark 1:15). There's no getting around His meaning here. One first has to come face-to-face with her need for salvation before she can receive this great gift. How can an infant make such a choice?

Also, it's critical to note that the Holy Spirit is given at the moment of repentance (Acts 2:38). In the Gospel of Mark, quoted above, we know for certain that God's timetable for obtaining salvation has begun.

Lord, I thank You that those who lived before Jesus came to earth were given the same Gospel message through the prophets. I thank You that You have always provided a way to salvation.

A Dance in the Fiery Furnace

"O peoples, nations and men of every language...
you are to fall down and worship the golden image
that Nebuchadnezzar the king has set up."

DANIEL 3:4–5

King Nebuchadnezzar had slipped into total egotism, making an image of gold that represented himself and then demanding worship from the people. The king's advisors used this proclamation to entrap Daniel's friends who refused to bow down to any king but the Lord. Therefore, Shadrach, Meshach, and Abednego were bound and then thrown into a fiery furnace.

But when the king looked into the furnace, he saw a fourth person in the midst of the fire. "Look! I see four men loosed and walking about in the midst of the fire without harm, and the appearance of the fourth is like a son of the gods!" (Daniel 3:25). So the king ordered them out again.

Jesus was with Daniel's friends in the fire.

Lord, be my faithful God, just as You were to Daniel's
friends. Keep me from harm as I walk
through the fires in my own life.

A True Mother's Love

"So give Your servant an understanding heart to judge
Your people to discern between good and evil.
For who is able to judge this great people of Yours?"

1 KINGS 3:9

Shortly after King Solomon had asked the Lord for wisdom, two harlots brought their case before him. Each woman stated that one particular infant belonged to her.

As they stood arguing and shouting, Solomon said, " 'Get me a sword.' So they brought a sword before the king. The king said, 'Divide the living child in two, and give half to the one and half to the other' " (1 Kings 3:24–25). Solomon knew that the child's true mother would come to the baby's defense.

Within minutes the issue was resolved and the real mother held her child again. "When all Israel heard of the judgment which the king had handed down, they feared the king, for they saw that the wisdom of God was in him to administer justice" (3:28).

Lord, how I pray that such wisdom would be given to
lawmakers. I also need Your guidance for my family.
Help me remember to turn to You in my dilemmas.

Saul and Stephen

*They went on stoning Stephen as he called on the Lord
and said, "Lord Jesus, receive my spirit!" Then falling on
his knees, he cried out with a loud voice, "Lord, do not hold
this sin against them!" Having said this, he fell asleep.
Saul was in hearty agreement with putting him to death.
And on that day a great persecution began
against the church in Jerusalem.*

ACTS 7:59–60; 8:1

After the stoning of Stephen, Saul entered home after
home and dragged Christians off to prison.

And then the powerful hand of the Lord God
intervened.

"Suddenly a light from heaven flashed around him;
and he fell to the ground and heard a voice saying to him,
'Saul, Saul, why are you persecuting Me?' And he said,
'Who are You, Lord?' And He said, 'I am Jesus whom you
are persecuting, but get up and enter the city, and it will be
told you what you must do'" (Acts 9:3–6).

Thank You, God, for changing Saul into Paul!

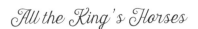

All the King's Horses

Solomon amassed chariots and horsemen.
2 CHRONICLES 1:14

Solomon's horses were the finest that money could buy. But they weren't just for pleasure. These valiant steeds helped defend his kingdom and also provided revenue as they were sold or loaned to other kings.

Solomon's horses were stationed in strategic cities, ready to guard and protect the kingdom. And in 1 Kings 4:26 we see that "Solomon had 40,000 stalls of horses for his chariots." He also had deputies who "brought barley and straw for the horses and swift steeds to the place where it should be, each according to his charge" (1 Kings 4:28).

Long before Israel even had a king, the Lord had established certain standards for this monarch. He was not to multiply horses for himself, nor cause the people to return to Egypt to get horses (Deuteronomy 17:14–16). God didn't want the king's heart to turn away from following Him.

*Had Solomon followed God's commands,
his kingdom would have been assured of survival.
Lord, help me to remain faithful.*

Antichrist, the Ruler to Come

"In his place a despicable person will arise, on whom the honor of kingship has not been conferred, but he will come in a time of tranquility and seize the kingdom by intrigue."

DANIEL 11:21

The antichrist is a real person who will one day deviously slither onto the scene right on cue. He will appear indispensable at a time of worldwide, unsolvable chaos. His allies will be the foes of God.

His deception will be so great that people will fail to see his face of evil until "The abomination of desolation" takes place (Matthew 24:15). Three and one-half years after he comes on the scene, the antichrist will enter the rebuilt temple in Jerusalem, declare himself god, and demand worship and allegiance from the world. Jesus Himself warned the Jews about this diabolical person, telling them that when they saw him "those who are in Judea must flee to the mountains" (Mark 13:14).

Lord, compel me with new urgency to study Your powerful Word, that I might bring it to others.

Michael Stands Guard

"Now at that time Michael, the great prince who stands guard over the sons of your people, will arise. And there will be a time of distress such as never occurred since there was a nation until that time; and at that time your people, everyone who is found written in the book, will be rescued."

DANIEL 12:1

Those whose names are written in the book will be spared. God writes the names in His book. It's called the Lamb's book of life.

It is these, whose names are written in the book, who will be rescued from destruction: "These are the ones who come out of the great tribulation, and they have washed their robes and made them white in the blood of the Lamb. For this reason, they are before the throne of God; and they serve Him day and night in His temple; and He who sits on the throne will spread His tabernacle over them" (Revelation 7:14–15).

Lamb of God, who takes away sin,
I want to know my name is written in Your book!

But What about the Jews?

For if Abraham was justified by works, he has something to boast about; but not before God. For what does the Scripture say? "ABRAHAM BELIEVED GOD, AND IT WAS CREDITED TO HIM AS RIGHTEOUSNESS."

ROMANS 4:2–3

Salvation is not based on our "goodness" but rather on Christ's. For no matter how diligently we try to keep those Ten Commandments, we're going to fail.

God made Abraham, the one the Jews claim as their father, a promise, and he believed God.

His belief wasn't merely an intellectual assent. The supreme God of the universe, who made absolutely everything that Abraham now saw in his world, not only had deigned to speak to him but had promised him an heir. The reason that Abraham could place his trust in God was because God kept His promises. No matter how impossible the situation looks, God always comes through.

I thank You that I worship a God whose Word can be trusted. I know Jesus will always be there for me.

Gomer, a Picture of Israel

The LORD said to Hosea, "Go, take to yourself a wife of harlotry and have children of harlotry; for the land commits flagrant harlotry, forsaking the LORD."
So he went and took Gomer the daughter of Diblaim, and she conceived and bore him a son.

HOSEA 1:2-3

Why would God ask the prophet Hosea to enter into an unwholesome alliance? Because He wanted Israel to understand what it was like to observe the one to whom they were betrothed go off and play the harlot. When Israel entered into the covenant with God, the people had promised fidelity to Him. But this beloved nation had "prostituted" themselves in worship of false gods, forsaking their true God.

The book of Hosea reveals the brokenness of God's own heart as He watched Israel wander away. Now God was forced to take action against the people He loved, in order to bring them back to Him.

"And I will say to those who were not My people,
'You are My people!'" (Hosea 2:23).
Lord, thank You for Your unique invitation.

Peace Despite Our Trials

Therefore, having been justified by faith, we have peace with God through our Lord Jesus Christ, through whom also we have obtained our introduction by faith into this grace in which we stand; and we exult in hope of the glory of God.... For while we were still helpless, at the right time Christ died for the ungodly.

ROMANS 5:1–2, 6

People have scoured every nook and cranny of the globe in search of peace. From yoga and transcendental meditation to new age tranquility tapes and self-empowerment courses, people will try just about anything. But do these methods work?

Of course not! Instead, each new road eventually leads to the dead ends of dissatisfaction and emptiness. "I have seen all the works which have been done under the sun, and behold, all is vanity and striving after wind" (Ecclesiastes 1:14). The promises of peace that this world has to offer are nothing more than vapors of an expensive fragrance.

Enduring tranquility cannot be found outside a relationship with Christ.

Lord, I know the only true and lasting peace comes from Jesus Christ.

The Fruit of the Spirit

But the fruit of the Spirit is love, joy, peace, patience, kindness, goodness, faithfulness, gentleness, self-control; against such things there is no law. Now those who belong to Christ Jesus have crucified the flesh with its passions and desires. If we live by the Spirit, let us also walk by the Spirit.

GALATIANS 5:22–25

When we become Christians, we receive spiritual gifts as a result of our inward relationship with Jesus Christ. These gifts are known in the Bible as the fruit of the Spirit, but what does that really mean?

Inventoried in today's scripture are qualities that, apart from God's power, would not likely be displayed in our character.

Why is God showering us with these gifts? Because they prove that He can enter a human life and bring about change, so that others might also be won to Christ as they observe this miracle.

Lord, my greatest gift from You is salvation;
Your grace enables me to begin life with a fresh start.
And with this transformation of character, spiritual fruit
becomes the yield, shared as I serve the body
of believers with my unique spiritual gifts.

Joel and a Plague of Locusts

What the gnawing locust has left, the swarming locust has eaten. . .and what the creeping locust has left, the stripping locust has eaten.

JOEL 1:4

Joel's words could provide a great plotline for a sci-fi thriller. Other catastrophes would follow.

The apostle Peter explained Pentecost in light of Joel's prophecy: "This is what was spoken of through the prophet Joel: 'AND IT SHALL BE IN THE LAST DAYS,' God says, 'THAT I WILL POUR FORTH OF MY SPIRIT. . . And they shall prophesy. AND I WILL GRANT WONDERS IN THE SKY ABOVE AND SIGNS ON THE EARTH BELOW. . .BEFORE THE GREAT AND GLORIOUS DAY OF THE LORD SHALL COME. AND IT SHALL BE THAT EVERYONE WHO CALLS ON THE NAME OF THE LORD WILL BE SAVED' " (Acts 2:16–21).

The information contained in the book of Joel is referred to as eschatology, or a study of the end times, and it parallels other passages in scripture. When Jesus spoke to His disciples, He, too, quoted this prophetic passage, providing additional clarity.

Lord, I rejoice in Your Word.

Paul's Prayer for the Jews

Brethren, my heart's desire and my prayer
to God for them is for their salvation.

ROMANS 10:1

Is the deepest concern of your heart that those whom you love will share heaven with Christ? The deepest longing of Paul's soul was that the Jews might know their Messiah.

Paul longed for the Israelites, "to whom belongs the adoption as sons, and the glory and the covenants and the giving of the Law and the temple service and the promises," to understand that Christ had come to save them (Romans 9:4).

The Jews couldn't truly be God's children until they partook of the light of truth. "For the Scripture says, 'WHOEVER BELIEVES IN HIM WILL NOT BE DISAPPOINTED.' For there is no distinction between Jew and Greek; for the same Lord is Lord of all, abounding in riches for all who call on Him; for 'WHOEVER WILL CALL ON THE NAME OF THE LORD WILL BE SAVED' " (Romans 10:11–13).

Lord, clarify Your Word,
that women and men may yield in faith.

Nehemiah and the Walls of Jerusalem

*"The remnant there in the province who survived
the captivity are in great distress and reproach,
and the wall of Jerusalem is broken down
and its gates are burned with fire."*

NEHEMIAH 1:3

Nehemiah records the events that took place as
Jerusalem's walls were repaired. Fortified walls were
necessary not only to guard the perimeter of the great city,
but also to demonstrate the renewed pride and unity of its
citizens.

Nehemiah requested that King Artaxerxes send
him to Judah that he might rebuild the walls. And all of
Nehemiah's time of fasting and prayer was answered as
the king wrote letters of safe passage for him to all "the
governors of the provinces beyond the River" (Nehemiah
2:7). In God's timing Nehemiah shared his plan with the
remnant of Israel.

*Lord, let me learn from Nehemiah's example.
Let me seek Your will through prayer and study,
never losing sight of Your Son.*

Joel Prophesies a Final Judgment

Hasten and come, all you surrounding nations,
and gather yourselves there. Bring down, O LORD,
Your mighty ones. Let the nations be aroused and
come up to the valley of Jehoshaphat, for there
I will sit to judge all the surrounding nations.

JOEL 3:11–12

Jerusalem will be the site of the world's last and greatest battle as all the surrounding nations rage against the Holy City. However, the powerful, almighty God of the universe will intervene on Israel's behalf.

"The LORD roars from Zion and utters His voice from Jerusalem, and the heavens and the earth tremble. But the LORD is a refuge for His people and a stronghold to the sons of Israel. Then you will know that I am the LORD your God, dwelling in Zion, My holy mountain. So Jerusalem will be holy, and strangers will pass through it no more" (Joel 3:16–17).

Lord, I don't like to consider the brutality of this final judgment. However, I know that You are fair and just and have given men and women ample time and warning to repent.

Renewing Our Minds

Present your bodies a living and holy sacrifice,
acceptable to God, which is your spiritual service of
worship. And do not be conformed to this world,
but be transformed by the renewing of your mind,
so that you may prove what the will of God is,
that which is good and acceptable and perfect.

ROMANS 12:1–2

Mary had lived an exemplary life and was betrothed to
Joseph. Then an angel came with an announcement that
would cast a shadow of doubt on her impeccable character.
God had asked Mary to bear His Son.

Leaving the results of this decision in the hands of her
powerful God, Mary accepted her role as the mother of the
Messiah. And during the difficult days that followed, she
allowed the Word of God to renew her mind.

Lord, I am grateful for Mary's example.

The Gathering at the Water Gate

And all the people gathered. . .at the square. . .and they asked Ezra the scribe to bring the book of the law of Moses which the Lord had given to Israel. Then Ezra the priest brought the law before the assembly. . .on the first day of the seventh month. He read from it before the square. . . and all the people were attentive to the book of the law.

NEHEMIAH 8:1–3

Through inspired teamwork, Nehemiah and the remnant of Israel finished rebuilding the wall in only fifty-two days (Nehemiah 6:15). Even their enemies lost the will to fight, recognizing this accomplishment as coming from the hand of Israel's God. Four times Sanballat and Geshem sent messages to Nehemiah, hoping to drag him away from finishing his task. And each time Nehemiah responded by saying, "I am doing a great work and I cannot come down" (6:3). Sanballat accused Nehemiah of appointing prophets to proclaim that a king was in Judah (6:7).

Still, Nehemiah refused to become agitated or frightened. Instead, he relied on God's strength.

Lord, let Nehemiah be an example of trust for me.

Amos the Prophet

Thus says the LORD, "For three transgressions of Damascus and for four I will not revoke its punishment."
AMOS 1:3

Throughout the Old Testament we've read accounts of God's wrath and fury directed toward those whom He loved who were flagrantly disobedient. But God also extended His loving hand of protection to those who walked in obedience.

Amos was a simple sheepherder from a small city about ten miles south of Jerusalem. He was called by God to deliver a warning to these stiff-necked, idol-worshipping people of the northern kingdom of Israel.

Contained within the nine chapters of this book is a list of the cities and peoples whom God considered ripe for judgment, along with the specific warnings. As angry as God already was, He still gave these people two years to repent before the great earthquake came. Still, the people refused to listen.

Lord, thank You for Amos's prophecy: "Also I will restore the captivity of My people Israel, and they will rebuild the ruined cities and live in them" (Amos 9:14).

Phoebe, Servant of the Church

I commend to you our sister Phoebe, who is a servant of the church which is at Cenchrea; that you receive her in the Lord in a manner worthy of the saints, and that you help her in whatever matter she may have need of you; for she herself has also been a helper of many, and of myself as well.

ROMANS 16:1–2

The apostle Paul singled Phoebe out as having been a great help both to the church at Cenchrea and to him personally. In bestowing this honor upon her, Paul showed to the ages the depth of Phoebe's Christian commitment.

Paul also requested that other believers receive Phoebe "in a manner worthy of the saints." Obviously Christ within her shone out to others like a beacon of light to a needy world. And he asked that they assist her. Some Bible translations also refer to her as a deaconess at the church in Cenchrea. At any rate, she was no ordinary woman.

Lord, let my life, as Phoebe's, shine before others.

The Apple of God's Eye

"For the day of the LORD draws near on all the nations.
As you have done, it will be done to you.
Your dealings will return on your own head."

OBADIAH 1:15

Obadiah is such a tiny Old Testament book that you've probably overlooked it. Yet there are prophecies and promises for Israel here that can't be missed.

Israel, the people God had chosen, began to feel so overconfident that they considered themselves invincible. But it wasn't God's choosing them that made them special. Instead, it was the protection of God that made them unique as a people. But now their arrogance and lack of true worship rendered them vulnerable to attack. Obadiah calls the people of Israel back to worship their God, but also issues a warning to Edom, the nation intent on wiping them out.

Lord, let me remember that it is Christ who is the head of His Church and I am but a member of the Body.

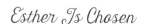

Esther Is Chosen

Then the king's attendants, who served him, said,
"Let beautiful young virgins be sought for the king."
ESTHER 2:2

The book of Esther is a beautiful story of a woman's absolute faith and trust in her God. God placed Esther in a position of authority in order to save the people of Israel.

Mordecai, a Jew in Susa, had returned from the Babylonian exile and was raising his orphaned niece, Esther. And she was "beautiful of form and face.... Esther was taken to the king's palace" (Esther 2:5–8).

Wisely, "Esther did not make known her people or her kindred" (2:10). Esther lived in the ultimate spa resort where, for over twelve months, she received beauty treatments and perfume baths.

Finally, "Esther was taken to King Ahasuerus.... The king loved Esther more than all the women, and she found favor and kindness with him. . .so that he set the royal crown on her head and made her queen instead of Vashti" (2:16–17).

In the beginning, Esther was unaware of how God would use her life. Lord, let me be as available and obedient to You.

Jonah Flees God's Call

The word of the LORD came to Jonah the son of Amittai
saying, "Arise, go to Nineveh the great city and cry
against it, for their wickedness has come up before
Me." But Jonah rose up to flee to Tarshish
from the presence of the LORD.

JONAH 1:1–3

Jonah flat out didn't want this job, no way, nohow! Therefore, he decided to get out of Dodge. And the quickest route happened to be on the next boat sailing.

God had solicited Jonah's help in bringing a message to Nineveh. However, Jonah's fear of these Ninevites loomed far greater than his fear of the Lord.

But God always gives men and women a chance to change, and so He set about the task of getting Jonah's attention in a way he'd never forget.

Lord, I know that finally Jonah responded in faith.
Please help me take responsibility for the areas
You're ready to work on in my life.

Hearing God's Spirit Speak

For to us God revealed them through the Spirit;
for the Spirit searches all things, even the depths of God....
Now we have received, not the spirit of the world,
but the Spirit who is from God, so that we may
know the things freely given to us by God.

1 CORINTHIANS 2:10, 12

To understand the things of God, you can't totally rely on what you received in your early education.

If you came to Christ as an adult, it's probably necessary to start from the beginning, using the Bible, not your memory. Find out what you believe and know why. If you never arrive at this understanding, how on earth can you share your faith with others?

Here's an excuse heard often: "We can't try to interpret the Bible ourselves because we'll get confused." But to refuse the Holy Spirit the opportunity to instruct you, as He promised He would, is to refuse true understanding.

Lord, fill my mind and heart with true understanding.

Esther Thwarts a Royal Plot

---

*In those days, while Mordecai was sitting at the king's gate,
Bigthan and Teresh, two of the king's officials from those
who guarded the door, became angry and sought to lay
hands on King Ahasuerus. But the plot became known
to Mordecai and he told Queen Esther, and Esther
informed the king in Mordecai's name.*

ESTHER 2:21–22

Overhearing a private conversation in which a murder plot
was discussed, Esther's uncle, Mordecai, a Jew, channeled
this information back to his niece, whom the king trusted.

An official, Haman, had been promoted shortly after
this incident had taken place. The king had commanded
that all who were at the king's gate bow down and pay
homage to Haman. However, Mordecai refused and
"Haman was filled with rage" (Esther 3:5).

Therefore, Haman set an evil plan in motion. Then
Haman talked the king into issuing a decree that this
people, the Jews, be destroyed.

*Lord, what a dark hour this was for Your people,
but You had already put a plan into action.*

Jonah Is Swallowed by a Great Fish

"Pick me up and throw me into the sea. Then the sea will become calm for you, for I know that on account of me this great storm has come upon you."

JONAH 1:12

The storm-tossed sailors have two options, and neither one sounds like the right one.

Although these men were mad at Jonah for involving them in his duel with God, they were also aware that tossing him overboard like unwanted cargo would almost certainly spell his death. It wasn't until they had no other option that they finally complied with his request.

As soon as they threw Jonah into the water, the sea stopped raging. "Then the men feared the LORD greatly, and they offered a sacrifice to the LORD and made vows. And the LORD appointed a great fish to swallow Jonah, and Jonah was in the stomach of the fish three days and three nights" (Jonah 1:16–17).

Lord, You alone have the ability to deliver a great fish to swallow a man whole and not harm him. Help me trust You for creative solutions to all my problems.

Our Bodies, God's Temple

*Do you not know that you are a temple of God
and that the Spirit of God dwells in you?*

1 CORINTHIANS 3:16

As we go about the business of life, perhaps it's hard to remember that God indwells us. The apostle Paul constantly wrestled with desiring to do the right thing but having his flesh at war with his spirit. "For I know that nothing good dwells in me, that is, in my flesh; for the willing is present in me, but the doing of the good is not. For the good that I want, I do not do, but I practice the very evil that I do not want" (Romans 7:18–19).

"However, you are not in the flesh but in the Spirit, if indeed the Spirit of God dwells in you. . . . If Christ is in you, though the body is dead because of sin, yet the spirit is alive because of righteousness" (8:9–10).

*Lord, let me live as though I believe
You are permeating my very being. Amen.*

The Need for Godly Judges

Does any one of you, when he has a case against his neighbor, dare to go to law before the unrighteous and not before the saints? Or do you not know that the saints will judge the world? If the world is judged by you, are you not competent to constitute the smallest law courts?

1 CORINTHIANS 6:1-2

God meant for His people to govern themselves so that true justice would be served. But He also intended that believers work out their differences in love. Today men and women have quit counting on the power of God to rule in their lives and have turned instead to the "courts of the unbelievers," where they have not found justice.

The verses above are meant to give you hope. For the saints of God will one day judge those who operate within this world's system of injustice. As God brings down His own pair of legal scales to weigh and measure, they will be held accountable to Him.

Lord, help me remember the meaning of justice. May my court of law be governed by Your Holy Spirit in my heart.

The First to View the Resurrection

Mary Magdalene came early to the tomb,
while it was still dark.

JOHN 20:1

Peter and John ran to the tomb, viewed the linen wrappings, and then left again (John 20:6–10). They left too soon, missing the miracle. "But Mary was standing outside the tomb weeping; and so, as she wept, she stooped and looked into the tomb; and she saw two angels. . . . And they said to her, 'Woman, why are you weeping?' She said to them, 'Because they have taken away my Lord, and I do not know where they have laid Him.' When she had said this, she turned around and saw Jesus standing there, and did not know that it was Jesus" (20:11–14).

She said to him, " 'Sir, if you have carried Him away, tell me where you have laid Him, and I will take Him away' " (20:15).

But then He said, "Mary!" (20:16). And the sound of His voice calmed her frantic fears, dried her tears, and warmed her heart.

Lord, many times I miss the miracle You
have already prepared. Open my eyes!

Esther Requests a New Law

On that day King Ahasuerus gave the house of Haman,
the enemy of the Jews, to Queen Esther; and Mordecai
came before the king, for Esther had disclosed what he
was to her. . . . And Esther set Mordecai over the house of
Haman. Then Esther spoke again to the king, fell at his feet,
wept and implored him to avert the evil scheme of Haman
the Agagite and his plot which he had devised against the
Jews. The king extended the golden scepter to Esther.
So Esther arose and stood before the king.

ESTHER 8:1–4

Esther and Mordecai were among the few in the king's
palace who had acted in the king's behalf. Everyone else
desired personal gain. Esther had risked her life not only
for her people but also for the king. Had it not been for
God's intervention, Haman undoubtedly would have
hanged Esther on that gallows right along with Mordecai.

Lord, I thank You for this account of Esther's
obedience, loyalty, and trust.

Micah Knew His God

Hear, O peoples, all of you; listen, O earth and all it contains, and let the Lord GOD be a witness against you, the Lord from His holy temple. For behold, the LORD is coming forth from His place. He will come down and tread on the high places of the earth.

MICAH 1:2–3

The events recorded in Micah would be fulfilled in the near and far-distant future.

"The mountains will melt under Him and the valleys will be split, like wax before the fire, like water poured down a steep place. All this is for the rebellion of Jacob and for the sins of the house of Israel. . . . For I will make Samaria a heap of ruins in the open country, planting places for a vineyard. I will pour her stones down into the valley and will lay bare her foundations" (Micah 1:4–6).

Why was God doing this to His people? Both Judah and Israel had forsaken their God, becoming steeped in idolatry.

Lord, keep me from following in the footsteps of the rebellious so that I might not require bitter lessons of truth.

The Preacher's Livelihood

Who at any time serves as a soldier at his own expense?
Who plants a vineyard and does not eat the fruit of it?
Or who tends a flock and does not use the milk of the flock?

1 CORINTHIANS 9:7

Those who bring us the Word of God deserve a living wage. This is the point Paul is making. After all, the apostles had given up their homes and any semblance of normal family life in order to travel and present the Gospel. "Do we not have a right to eat and drink? Do we not have a right to take along a believing wife, even as the rest of the apostles and the brothers of the Lord and Cephas? Or do only Barnabas and I not have a right to refrain from working?" (1 Corinthians 9:4–6).

The word *apostle* means "one sent under commission." And if they had been called into service by God, weren't they entitled to financial support from the body of believers?

Lord, let me remember in my prayers, tithes,
and offerings all those who labor to bring the
Word of God to me and others.

The Reason for Job's Suffering

*Job. . .was blameless, upright, fearing God and turning
away from evil. Seven sons and three daughters were born
to him. His possessions also were 7,000 sheep,
3,000 camels, 500 yoke of oxen, 500 female
donkeys, and very many servants.*

JOB 1:1–3

Satan intimated to God that Job only loved Him because
of all the blessings Job had received. "Then the LORD said
to Satan, 'Behold, all that he has is in your power, only do
not put forth your hand on him' " (Job 1:12).

Job's life became an unwelcome ride on a trolley
called tragedy. In one day he lost all his children and his
house, servants, and livestock. And through all of this, Job
refused to blame God or sin.

*Lord, as a Christian, lead me so that I do not expect
You to be my "celestial Santa Claus." Lead me so
I continue to follow, no matter the circumstances.*

The Content of Our Thoughts

Woe to those who scheme iniquity,
who work out evil on their beds!
MICAH 2:1-2

Micah acknowledges that the source of evil thoughts is the human mind. Other portions of scripture also bear out this truth.

"Transgression speaks to the ungodly within his heart; there is no fear of God before his eyes. For it flatters him in his own eyes concerning the discovery of his iniquity and the hatred of it. The words of his mouth are wickedness and deceit; he has ceased to be wise and to do good. He plans wickedness upon his bed; he sets himself on a path that is not good; he does not despise evil" (Psalm 36:1-4).

Therein lies the problem, that we at some point begin to accept wickedness as good. And the things we devise in our minds then become the vehicle for our actions.

Lord, guard my mind from evil that I might not ruminate
on such things and be propelled into ungodly actions.

God, Judge of Immorality

Now these things happened as examples for us, so that
we would not crave evil things as they also craved. . . .
Nor let us act immorally, as some of them did,
and twenty-three thousand fell in one day.

1 CORINTHIANS 10:6, 8

By reading the entire Bible, we have the privilege of learning from God's dealings with men and women throughout recorded history so we will not fall into the same traps. Twenty-three thousand people fell by the sword in one day because they joined themselves with pagan gods in sexual rituals, refusing to obey the true God.

How can we stop ourselves from falling into sin? By remembering: "No temptation has overtaken you but such as is common to man; and God is faithful, who will not allow you to be tempted beyond what you are able, but with the temptation will provide the way of escape also, so that you will be able to endure it" (1 Corinthians 10:13).

Father, help me avoid temptation by taking
one step closer to You.

The Holy Spirit, Our Great Gift

Therefore I make known to you that no one speaking by
the Spirit of God says, "Jesus is accursed"; and no one
can say, "Jesus is Lord," except by the Holy Spirit.

1 CORINTHIANS 12:3

For twenty-nine years I waded through the motions of life, wondering whether the Creator really cared for me at all.

It's no accident that despair caused me to succumb to messages of doubt concerning God's nature and character. The evil one is, after all, the author of confusion and lies. However, as I tested the spirits, the truth became clear. "By this you know the Spirit of God: every spirit that confesses that Jesus Christ has come in the flesh is from God; and every spirit that does not confess Jesus is not from God; this is the spirit of the antichrist, of which you have heard that it is coming, and now it is already in the world" (1 John 4:2–3).

Lord, I know if I'm listening to a message that makes me depressed and defeated, it's from Satan. I know the one that says I'm worth dying for is from Christ.

God Has Been There, Done That

"It is God who removes the mountains. . .who alone stretches out the heavens and tramples down the waves of the sea."

JOB 9:5, 8

In one theology class I took, the teacher asked us to examine the ways in which we attempt to stuff God into a box. As A. W. Tozer said, "We tend to reduce God to manageable terms."

As our human nature cries out to control what we don't understand, this feat becomes impossible. For the God who has created all that we see, hear, touch, taste, and smell has been there and done that. When we accept this, our own importance seems diminished.

Even as Job screamed for relief from his pain, he recognized that both blessings and testing through trials flowed from the same loving hands (Job 10:8–9, 12).

I await the balm of good news from You, Lord. "
O may Your lovingkindness comfort me,
according to Your word to Your servant.
May Your compassion come to me that I may live,
for Your law is my delight" (Psalm 119:76–77).

What Response Does God Require?

With what shall I come to the LORD and bow myself before the God on high?... He has told you, O man, what is good; and what does the LORD require of you but to do justice, to love kindness, and to walk humbly with your God?

MICAH 6:6, 8

Christ has already paid the price that needed to be exacted for our sins. He took the whips, the lashes, the nailing to the cross, the verbal rebukes, and also the physical agony on our behalf. The God of this universe looked upon our futility and became a man, and then He sacrificed His life so that we who did not and could not ever deserve His mercy might obtain it. Jesus Christ did all this because He is both just and kind.

Though I expend every effort, I can never rid myself of sin. You've already provided the only way in which I can be cleansed.

His Fortunes Restored

*The LORD restored the fortunes of Job when he prayed for
his friends, and the LORD increased all that Job had
twofold.... The LORD blessed the latter days of Job
more than his beginning; and he had 14,000 sheep and
6,000 camels and 1,000 yoke of oxen and 1,000 female
donkeys. He had seven sons and three daughters.*

JOB 42:10, 12–13

Don't you just love stories with happy endings? Reading
through the book of Job makes anyone cry out for a great
finish.

In today's scripture, we join up again with Job's two
friends. Well, the long arm of God's justice finally caught
up with them and the Lord called them to accountability
(Job 42:8).

Finally, Job received the Lord's public vindication.
Revenge doesn't get any sweeter than that! And don't you
know that Eliphaz, Bildad, and Zophar were sweatin' it
big-time as they awaited Job's eloquent prayer that would
restrain God's hand of wrath!

*Lord, through Job's pain, agony, and loss You placed
"wisdom in his innermost being" concerning deep and
marvelous truths about Your character (Job 38:36).
When I am afflicted, remind me to turn toward You.*

Nahum Proclaims Israel's Restoration

Behold, on the mountains the feet of him who brings good news, who announces peace! Celebrate your feasts, O Judah; pay your vows. For never again will the wicked one pass through you; he is cut off completely.

NAHUM 1:15

No news could be sweeter than the confirmation that a mighty enemy army was about to suffer a great demise. God gave Nahum, the prophet, just such a vision concerning the great Assyrian invaders who had devastated Judah. It had been such a long time that these pagans began boasting that no god would be able to deliver the Israelites. However, the true God of power and might was now ready to act against them for enslaving His people. And they never saw it coming!

*Lord, You are a mighty foe indeed!
Why do people devise plots against You?*

When Will Our Suffering Cease?

Blessed be the God and Father of our Lord Jesus Christ,
the Father of mercies and God of all comfort, who comforts
us in all our affliction so that we will be able to comfort
those who are in any affliction with the comfort with which
we ourselves are comforted by God. . . . But if we
are afflicted, it is for your comfort and salvation.

2 CORINTHIANS 1:3-4, 6

My son, an experienced mountain biker and triathlete, hit some debris in the street when he was riding recently and was thrown from his bike and onto a pile of bricks. His knee required surgery to repair the breaks.

He and his fiancée have learned to depend upon each other in a new way: she is providing the medical expertise, while he has learned to allow her to intervene. And both of them depend entirely on the Lord's sufficiency.

This is the purpose of our trials, that we might comfort one another and lean on the Lord's strength.

Thank You, God, that in heaven all suffering will cease.

What Is Your Foundation?

*"Woe to him who builds a city with bloodshed
and founds a town with violence!"*

HABAKKUK 2:12

Martin Luther was pierced by a verse in Habakkuk, and
his reaction changed the course of church history. "The
righteous will live by his faith" (Habakkuk 2:4). But in
whom is this faith placed? If our faith is in Christ, we
are established upon firm ground. But if it's in systems,
programs, or even religion, it's doomed to fail.

The people of Judah were entering their darkest hour.
The Babylonians had invaded this southern kingdom
three times. During the final siege, both Jerusalem and the
temple were destroyed. Habakkuk is seeking assurance
from the Lord that He will save them from extinction.

*Thank You, God, for Your promise to Habakkuk:
"For the vision is yet for the appointed time;
it hastens toward the goal and it will not fail.
Though it tarries, wait for it; for it will certainly
come, it will not delay" (Habakkuk 2:3).*

Paul's Trip to Paradise

I know a man in Christ who fourteen years ago. . .was caught up into Paradise and heard inexpressible words, which a man is not permitted to speak. On behalf of such a man I will boast; but on my own behalf I will not boast, except in regard to my weaknesses.

2 CORINTHIANS 12:2, 4-5

God propelled Paul up to heaven for a glimpse of what was ahead for him and all believers.

But why does Paul present this vision as though it happened to someone else? Remember that he had been trained as a rabbi and had received a thorough knowledge of the law. Rabbis often refer to themselves in the third person to refrain from sounding unduly prideful.

Lord, Your magnificent presence is all I need to provide me with the momentum to continue spreading Your Word.

Who Is the Rightful Heir?

*Abraham had two sons, one by the bondwoman and one
by the free woman. But the son by the bondwoman
was born according to the flesh, and the son by
the free woman through the promise.*

GALATIANS 4:22-23

God had promised Abraham a son, but at eighty-six years
old, Abraham had become weary of waiting (Genesis
16:16). To him, it was apparent that Sarah, his wife, was
barren. So at Sarah's urging, Abraham sought out her
slave girl Hagar, and she conceived. Abraham's action
led to much dissension within his home. And by the time
Sarah conceived the son of promise, the household was in
a complete upheaval. God promised to make both sides
great nations (Genesis 21:9–13).

   Paul now uses these two sons to illustrate the status of
the unbeliever versus her changed relationship once she
commits her life to Christ. Once we were slaves to sin, but
with our redemption in Christ we become free.

*Lord, through the line of Isaac men and women are truly
blessed. For Christ Himself would be that seed from whom
redemption would come (Galatians 3:13 –18).*